The Complete Guide to Pet Daycare

The Complete Guide to Pet Daycare

Edgar Perkins

MURPHY & MOORE
www.murphy-moorepublishing.com

The Complete Guide to Pet Daycare
Edgar Perkins
ISBN: 978-1-63987-525-2 (Hardback)

MURPHY & MOORE

Published by Murphy & Moore Publishing,
1 Rockefeller Plaza,
New York City, NY 10020, USA

Cataloging-in-Publication Data

The complete guide to pet daycare / Edgar Perkins.
     p. cm.
Includes bibliographical references and index.
ISBN 978-1-63987-525-2
1. Pet sitting--Vocational guidance. 2. Pets--Services for--Vocational guidance.
3. Pet industry--Vocational guidance. I. Perkins, Edgar.
SF414.34 .C66 2022
636.088 7--dc23

For more information regarding Murphy & Moore Publishing and its products, please visit the publisher's website www.murphy-moorepublishing.com

Table of Contents

Preface

Pet daycares are centers that provide care to pets. Services provided to pets at a pet daycare include grooming, spa services, boarding services, food, games and exercise, discipline, etc. It is important that the pets are placed in an environment that is animal-friendly and relaxed. Pet sitting is a related concept where pet care services are based out of the home. For someone with an interest and eye for detail, this book covers the most significant topics in the field of professional pet care and management. This book attempts to assist those with a goal of delving into this field.

A short introduction to every chapter is written below to provide an overview of the content of the book:

Chapter 1- Pet sitting is the care service that is provided to pets. Promoting the business, getting a license and getting insurance are important tasks that need to be done. This is an introductory chapter which will introduce briefly all the significant aspects of pet sitting; **Chapter 2-** Pet day care centers provide training to animals, especially dogs and cats. Being firm and providing rewards and treats are important while training pets. They can be trained to respond to specific stimuli. This chapter elucidates the crucial theories and principles of pet training; **Chapter 3-** Giving care to pets is a primary task of pet daycare centers. Being updated about each pet's needs and requirements, such as diet and exercise is very important. Providing first aid, if necessary, is also crucial. The topics discussed in the chapter are of great importance to broaden the existing knowledge on pet care; **Chapter 4-** Pets require cleaning and grooming. Keeping the surroundings clean where the pet primarily stays is also important. Hygiene is also important for keeping diseases as well as parasites at bay. The aspects elucidated in this chapter are of vital importance, and provide a better understanding of pet grooming.

I extend my sincere thanks to the publisher for considering me worthy of this task. Finally, I thank my family for being a source of support and help.

Edgar Perkins

Pet Sitting

Pet Sitting is care service provided to pets. Most often, pet sitting involves a pet sitting professional taking charge of a pet at the owner's home or any other designated place. This introductory chapter focuses on the various aspects of pet sitting.

Pet Sitting

A pet sitter is a contracted service provider who takes care of a pet or other animal at its own home rather than at a designated care facility or other house.

Professional Industry

The professional pet-sitting industry is growing rapidly with numbers over 25,000 being reported because many pet owners feel that there are advantages to using pet sitters, rather than traditional pet care options. Reasons people use pet sitters include:

- Possible reduced stress on pets because pets are cared for in their own homes,

- No "travel trauma" to pets because they do not need to be transported anywhere,

- Exposure to illnesses and parasites of other animals is minimized,

- Required vaccinations are often less restrictive than those necessary at a kennel,

- Pets stay on their regular routines and do not need to adapt to a new environment,

- Not having to deal with neighbors, friends or family members feeling that they are inconvenienced,

- Convenience for pets with health problems and mobility issues due to arthritis, dysplasia, incontinence, etc.

New businesses owners are attracted to the industry because of the large number of pet owners in many industrialized countries, as well as the low input cost and entry barrier to the industry.

Professional pet sitters are often licensed, and insured for liability including care, custody, and control of the pets in their care. Many pet sitters are also bonded or insured for theft. Pet sitters usually have training, such as pet first aid certification, animal husbandry classes, or pet sitting accreditation. A number of professional organizations exist to help pet sitters improve their services. It is not entirely uncommon for pet sitters to be interviewed prior to being given the job.

In many areas, no special occupational license is required for pet sitters. The term "licensed" is often used by pet sitting professionals to refer to licenses to do business, kennel licenses, and/or animal transportation permits available within the coverage area of the business. These licenses may or may not be required, depending on the location. Licenses are not available in all areas.

The gig economy has led to the creation of various apps and websites to match pet-sitters with clients.

Services

There are many different services which can be offered by pet sitters.

Vacation Care

During vacation pet sitting, a pet sitter visits a client's home several times, as required. The exact length of visit is determined by both pet owners and pet sitters, averaging from fifteen to forty-five minutes. Typical services offered include: providing the pets' customary diet and exercise routine, administration of medications, vitamins, and other special care, monitoring health and arranging for medical treatment in case of illness. Most pet sitters bill clients on a per-visit or per-day basis, including additional charges for multiple pets, travel expenses, and special tasks. Less commonly, pet sitters offer live-in care. Pet sitters also provide house sitting in conjunction with vacation pet care.

Dog Walking

Pet sitters also commonly provide dog walking services. Disabled clients and the elderly often hire pet sitters to exercise and care for their pets if they are unable to do so.

Pet sitters may also offer other more aggressive methods of exercise for dogs during dog walking appointments. These may include jogging, running, inline skating, bicycling, or dog scootering with client dogs.

Commercial dog walkers in a very limited number of regions are required to obtain license for dog walking along with inspection of vehicle that is used to transport dogs for commercial walking and limitation over the number of dogs that can be walked at one time.

Additional Services

Some pet sitters may also offer additional pet services, such as dog boarding, dog grooming, or veterinarian care. These additional industries are often subject to special regulations and licensing requirements.

Insurance and Bonding

Insurance

Most professional pet sitters are insured through Pet Sitter insurance providers. Most Pet Sitting insurance providers are country specific, and currently are limited primarily to the United Kingdom, the United States, Australia, and Canada.

As of 2016, the major American and Canadian pet sitting liability insurance providers include claim limits from 2 million to 4 million or higher per claim for liability claims. They also include an uncommon endorsement that provides coverage for care, custody, and control of the client pets from $10,000 to $200,000 per occurrence. Coverage is included for fire damage, lost keys, and other negligence claims. The major UK pet sitting insurance providers claim coverage limits between £2,000,000 and £10,000,000. The limits for liability claims generally range from £2,000,000 to £5,000,000.

Most pet sitter insurance plans provide coverage for pet transport. The majority of pet sitting industry insurers also provide care, custody, and control liability coverage for all animals, excluding loss from income from an animal that may be used for other business ventures such as farming.

Some resources recommend that pet sitters be bonded. That recommendation has been dismissed by many professional organizations in recent years.

Bonding

A dishonesty or fidelity bond claim generally applies when a pet sitter is convicted in criminal court of theft from a client home. When the pet sitter is convicted, the bond will reimburse the client for the loss, and then seek reimbursement from the pet sitter. This process can take many years to complete, and usually relies on a criminal law court conviction.

Many pet sitters have decided to seek actual insurance coverage for theft instead of procuring a bond. Theft insurance coverage does not require convictions, and can include coverage for accidental breakage, mysterious disappearance, and accidental damage to items in a client home.

Other Insurance Topics

Pet sitters are generally not protected from injury to themselves by regular pet sitting liability coverage. Pet sitter liability insurance usually covers injury to other people and other pets.

Certification and Accreditation

A variety of pet sitting organizations offer optional training, testing, or review of credentials for pet sitters in the form of certification or accreditation. The curriculum of pet sitting programs may include pet care, health and first aid, animal law information, nutrition and behavior, and/or business development and management.

Certification that is credentials-based may require the pet sitter to provide a criminal background check, proof of insurance, proof of bonding, certificate of completion of a pet first aid program, documentation of business methods and policies, or other evidence to support their professionalism and adherence to minimum pet sitting industry standards.

It is common for pet sitters to obtain separate certification specifically in pet first aid. Hands-on pet first aid and CPR training classes are offered through such well known organizations in the U.S. such as the Red Cross, as well as through many private businesses specializing in pet first aid training. Virtual classes are also available for pet sitters who do not have hands-on classes available in their area.

How to Start a Pet Sitting Business

Starting your own pet sitting business is one of the most rewarding and profitable home businesses you can start. It doesn't take a lot of money to get started, and can be completely free if you use services such as Lodge Your Dog, you just need a love of animals. This article will show you how to get your own pet sitting business started, and gives some tips on making it successful.

Steps

1. Plan your business. All businesses, great and small, can benefit from a thoughtfully-written business plan. Here are some key points to consider:

- Analyze your market. How many people in your area might use a pet sitting service, and how many pet sitters are already in business in your area?

- Define your company. What will you do, specifically? If there's only one of you to start, you'll need to think about how and what you can actually do. What are the key benefits of your company, and what needs will it satisfy?

- Build a better mousetrap. What will make your company better than the competition? On-call pet pickup? Individual service? A name within the community, maybe with animal charities or shelters that gives you some credentials? What makes your business special?

- Develop a marketing campaign. How will you get the word out, and entice people to call you? Marketing yourself effectively is key to making your business successful, if your a pet sitter or an accountant! Given two identical companies, one with average marketing, and one with excellent marketing, the one with excellent marketing will virtually always win.

- Don't forget sales! Marketing is what makes people aware of your company. Sales is what brings them in the door. Don't neglect that part.

- Define your workflow. How will you fill your day with pet sitting, and how will you handle the inevitable emergency job, or the 2-hour-late pickup? How will you hire? What is the threshold for new employees?

- Develop a backup plan to cover all sits should you have an emergency that prevents you from taking care of the animals.

- What do you need to get started? Leashes? Cages? A big yard? Lots of kibbles and bits? You may not need a lot of cash to get started, but you will need some to gather supplies and pay for sales and marketing efforts.

- Where will you get funding? This might be from your savings, or an interested friend. It could be from the local shelter, or from your Uncle Moneybags.

- Show them the numbers. Before you take any funding—even from yourself—know what you will do with it, and how much is enough.

- Put your best foot forward. Describe your qualifications, and include anything that might be relevant to people trusting you with their pets. You might be a dog whisperer, or voted person most likely to herd cats. Make that known!

2. Name your business. If you want, you can give your business a name. Try to choose something unique that describes your business. Avoid cutesy or cliched names like "Pampered Pets." Consider a name that will be easily memorable and will tie you to your community.

3. Consider getting licensed. If you just wish to create a small "business" in your neighborhood or among family friends, you can skip this step. However, if you want to become a truly recognized

business, you may need to obtain a Business License (depending on your location) Go to https://www.sba.gov/content/what-state-licenses-and-permits-does-your-business-need if that's relevant, or look elsewhere on line to find out if your state or location requires a license.

4. Prepare the paperwork. You will need a service contract for your clients to sign. You will need a report card to record what you did during visits. You will need a way to track medications you may need to administer, you will need instruction sheets on how to take care of the pets and the home. Prepare these and any other necessary paperwork before opening the business.

5. Determine your rates. Consider how much money you want to charge. Try to keep your prices straight and to the point so as not to confuse your clients. Some factors to consider when creating prices:

- Type of animal. A dog is going to require more work than a fish, and thus you may want to charge more.

- Amount of time. How long do you have to watch the animals?

- Number of animals. How many animals are you taking care of?

6. Join a trade association. This means you will have support and advice when needed and you will work to a code of conduct which will give you business credibility.

- Distance from your headquarters. If you are going to service a larger area, you may want to do a mileage surcharge.

7. Build a website. In today's world people go straight to the Internet when they want to find a product or service. You will definitely increase you chances of success by using a website.

- Just having a website is not enough. In addition to being found your website has to tell people that you will care for and love their pets just like they do when they aren't home.

- People who use pet sitters really love their pets like their children and if you don't have the right message on your website it can kill your business before it ever gets started.

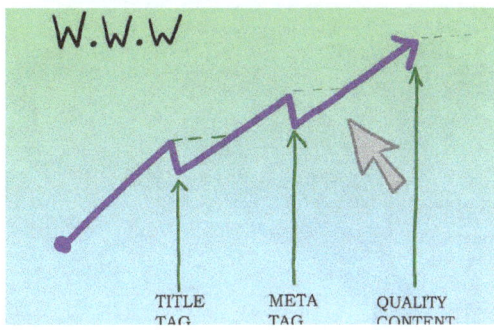

8. Optimize your site: simply publishing your site is no guarantee it will be found! Utilize these tips that Google recommends you follow in order to best optimize your pet sitting website:

- Title Tag: One of the most important elements when it comes to search engine optimization is your title tag. Make sure it contains your targeted keywords and is no more than 70 characters long. Some possibilities are:

  o Top pet sitter in Portland, OR, 20+ yrs experience! Call 503.555.1234

  o Pet sitting while you work! Call Willa Kenzie today, 503.555.1212

  o Away on business? Trust your pets to Willa Kenzie, 503.555.1212

- Meta tag: Inside your HTML code is your meta tag. Use accurate, normal language to describe your page content. Each page's meta tag should contain a unique description.

- Quality Content: At the end of the day, your website should give the visitor good quality content. Google rewards quality content that is unique and fresh. Update your site with new content often.

  o Once you have a website up and running, and are refreshing it regularly, consider signing up for Google AdSense, and running pet-related advertisements on your site for some extra income.

9. Open your doors for business. Once you have all your ducks in a row, start taking clients, and give them the service they signed up for—and give it your all.

10. Meet and greet your clients. Make sure you meet the owner as well as the pet before you

actually sit the pet. Ask about the pet's food, when to feed it, as well as what to give. What they're allowed to do, but don't ask simple questions such as "Is she allowed to potty on the couch?" or "Do I have to shut the gate when he is outside?" as it may make you seem unable to care for the pet or pets in question and could drive away customers, now and in the future.

- Make sure the pet has had all of it's shots as well as if it needs any medication and if so, when. Also, this would be the time to make any special arrangements.

- Always follow up with customers. When you first meet them, ask how they found you. If you find that there's one place in particular where customers are finding you, increase your exposure there.

- When the job is done, ask for feedback about what they liked, and what they could do better.

- When it gets to be too busy, hire an assistant, and then keep growing!

How to be a Good Pet Sitter

Pet-sitting can be a very rewarding and profitable way to earn your income. You will be responsible for caring for the pet while the owner is away, either for the day or for longer periods of time. As a pet sitter, you will play with the pet, feed them, brush them, and give them any medications or injections they might need. The pet's owner should feel they are leaving their pet in good hands with you.

Part 1

Preparing for a Pet Sitting Job

1. Make sure the position is right for you. Being a pet sitter is a rewarding but challenging experience. Before taking on a job, make sure you have the qualifications necessary to excel.

- A love of animals is perhaps the most important qualification a pet sitter can have. As you'll be spending the bulk of your time with your client's animals, make sure you genuinely enjoy animal company.

- Low stress is another desirable quality in a pet sitter. Your schedule will likely be subject to change as it depends heavily on the schedules of your clients. You need to be the type that's flexible and calm regarding sudden changes.

- Self motivation and organization are also desirable qualities for pet sitters. You'll need to manage your schedule around multiple clients and track the needs of a variety of cats, dogs, and other pets.

2. Get liability insurance. Professional pet sitters usually have commercial liability insurance to cover any accidents or incidents while they pet sit. If you're looking into longterm pet sitting, liability insurance might be a good investment.

- Pet sitting insurance will cover you in the event of any damage caused to the client's home, such as accidentally knocking over an expensive vase or breaking a window. It will also cover you if you lose grip of the dog's lead and he attacks another dog or person.

- In the United States, membership fees vary from company to company. Websites like petsitters.org and petsittersinsurance.com will help you compare rates and find the coverage that's right for you.

- If you're working through a pet sitting company, it's doubtful you'll need to take out insurance on your own. Most companies have policies in place that protect their employees. Check with the company you work for and ask questions about insurance and your personal coverage.

3. Consider pet sitting training. While a certification is not a requirement to be a pet sitter, having some professional training on your resume can impress present and future clients. It can also open up additional opportunities for you down the road.

- A certification of training lets clients know you're serious about your job and dedicated to providing the best care possible. If you ever want to work with a pet sitting agency, having some form of professional training is a great resume booster.

- A variety of organizations provide training programs for pet sitters. The National Assembly of Professional Pet Sitters and Pet Sitters International provide general training for pet sitting.

- The International Boarding and Pet Services Association provides training if you're looking into boarding dogs at your own kennel facility for extended periods. This can get pricey, however, as you're required to pass master exam to get certified. The exam can cost upwards of $125.

Part 2

Meeting with the Pet Owner

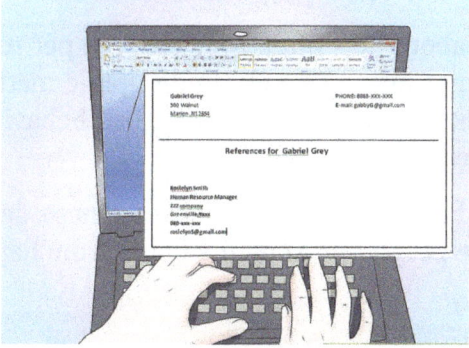

1. Provide references for past pet sitter jobs. Provide phone numbers and contact information for owners you have pet sit for in the past. This will show the owner you have experience as a pet sitter and are confident in your ability to take care of someone else's pet.

- Always ask permission before sharing someone's contact information. Make sure past clients agree to sever as your reference and get their preferred phone number and email.

- If possible, choose people you have worked with for a long time. For most jobs, a reference should ideally be someone you've known for a year to a year and a half.

- If you're new to the field and have never pet sat before, you can use past employers or friends whose animals you watched while they were on vacation.

2. Discuss expectations and needs. The pet's owner will have a variety of expectations of you, the

pet sitter, based around their pet's specific needs. Make sure all expectations are clearly stated and understood.

- Knowing the basics is important. Know where the pet's food is kept, how much they need each day, when and where to feed them, and any medications they're taking.

- Time commitment is another expectation that should be understood right away. For some jobs, you'll be required to stay in the owner's home. For others, you might only need to check in daily or every other day.

- Ask questions. It's your job as a good pet sitter to make sure all bases are covered, so have a running list of questions to ask pet owners. How old is the pet? What is their medical history? Do they do well with children? Other animals? How often should the dog be taken out? How often should a cat's litter box be changed? These are questions that should be addressed before the pet sitting job begins.

- Check with the owner about how often they give the pet treats or rewards, based on the pet's behavior. The owner may have certain discipline methods for the pet that they will expect you to follow, like withholding treats for bad behavior or acknowledging good behavior with a special treat.

- Ask the owner about the pet's likes and dislikes. These details will prepare you for any possible triggers for the pet and prevent any issues from happening to the pet while she is in your care.

3. Get all necessary contact information. Certain information is important in the event of an emergency or medical issue.

- Most owners will readily provide contact information for their veterinarian. Make sure you know where this information is written down. It might be a safe bet to enter contact information into your phone or have an electronic copy in your email in the event paper copies gets lost.

- In addition to the owner's contact information, ask for the phone number of a friend or family member close by. This way, in the event you can't contact the owner, you have a second person to contact in case of emergency.

4. Determine pay. If you're pet sitting for a friend or family member, pay may not be an issue. However, if this is a more professional endeavor you can expect to be paid and should determine the amount before the job begins.

- Research fees to see what is reasonable. Care.com is a great resource to research rates and fees associated with pet sitting in your area.

- The national average wage for pet sitters is $16/hour. So if you are working eight hours a day, at $16/hour, you can make $128/day. The owner may pay you a weekly wage. The average is around $600/week. You may also receive extra money for extra services, like house cleaning and maintenance, or payment in the form of free food and lodgings.

- Rates also go up depending on the number of pets you're caring for and your level of experience. The owner might want to negotiate fees. Make sure you are courteous during this process. You don't want to lose a client by being argumentative.

5. Meet the pet beforehand. If possible, schedule a practice visit. This way, the pet is familiar with you beforehand and you'll know where to find food, water, treats, and toys.

- Even if you already know the pet, a practice visit isn't a bad idea. There may be information about the pet that's never come up in casual conversation that you need to know as a pet sitter.

- The owner will also want to make sure the pet is comfortable with you. If there are any issues with aggression or timidness in your presence, they may want to select an alternative pet sitter. Do not take this personally. Sometimes a pet and person simply clash. Rescue pets often have negative associations that the owners do not fully understand, and you may inadvertently trigger a bad reaction.

Part 3
Caring for the Pet

1. Follow the schedule the owner provided. The owner likely left you both written and verbal instructions for pet care and upkeep.

- Feed the pet at the right time and give them the right amount of food. Cat owners sometimes let their cats have open access to dry food throughout the day. If this is the case, make sure to fill food bowls when they're running low and make sure clean water is provided.

- Give the pet any medications she needs. Pets who are on medications usually need to stick to a regular schedule and dosage. Follow the owner's instructions on how to give the pet her medication and don't forget or neglect the pet's medication.

- Clean litter boxes regularly and let dog's out as many times a day as the owner recommends.

2. Do some work in addition to pet sitting. If you want to stand out from other pet sitters, doing

some extra tasks for the owner can be a great way to show your added dedication.

- Do some basic upkeep for the pet owner's home, if you are pet sitting at their home. Water the plants. Collect the mail. Keep the home clean.

- While doing dishes might seem like a great way to earn favor, be careful. People often have specific organizational structures for their kitchens and might feel peeved if you mess with their system. If you do dishes, wash them, leave them out to dry, but refrain from putting them away.

3. Give the pet extra attention. A big part of your role as a pet sitter is to keep the pet safe and comfortable while her owner is away. The pet is likely nervous without their owner present so show them affection and attention on a daily basis.

- If the pet has a favorite toy, play with them often. It's best to play with the pet until the appear to run out of energy and lose interest in the game. This way, they'll be tired when you leave and more likely to sleep and relax until you return.

- After you fulfill duties like cleaning and feeding, sit with the pet and show them affection via stroking, cuddling, and talking. Pets, cats and dogs especially, are very social and crave human interaction when their owners are missing.

- Be careful about bringing in outside food and treats. The owner might have the pet on a specific diet and you don't want to disrupt that while away. Never give a pet table scraps without the owner's consent.

How to Advertise Dog Walking

In order for your small business to stand out amongst the competition, you must learn how to market it effectively. An effective advertisement grabs customers' attention and has them contacting you for your business. While there are several different ways to get the word out about your dog walking business, it helps to utilize a variety of advertising techniques targeted towards different customers.

Method 1

Using the Internet to Advertise

1. Post ads on the internet. You could try posting your advertisements on Craigslist or another website like MerchantCircle, GoogleMaps, or PetSitter.com. You can post ads by creating an online account, which allows you to revise or edit any online ads you post. If you post an ad without an account, it is more difficult to manage your personalized ads. Include a small paragraph of information about yourself to let new customers know your background and love for animals. State in your ad how long you have been doing this type of work, and why they should choose your services over another dog walking service.

- Make your listing stand out from others. You can accomplish this in many different ways. One way is to capitalize important words and frame these words with asterisks. Use a catchy headline to grab the reader's attention. A good example would be, "New Customers RECEIVE 50 PERCENT off DOG WALKING Services."

- Repost your ad every two days. Craigslist has rules and regulations to keep spam posts limited. This is why you are advised to post only once every two days.

- If you are underage, you might want to have a parent or trusted adult answer the replies so that they can talk to the person and decide if it is safe for you or not.

2. Make variations of your ad. Change your advertisement up by adding different worded ads to

attract different kinds of customers. Keep specific types of customers in mind as you design different ads targeted towards different people.

- For example, make ads for new customers, different ads for returning customers, and ads for people with more than one dog.

- Be sure to edit your ads for different target audiences. If you are writing an advertisement for PetSitter.com, you might want to emphasize your diverse pet watching skills, rather than just mentioning dog walking. If you are writing an advertisement for customers for with more than one pet, you should consider offering a discount.

3. Make yourself a website to advertise your services. The website is a great way to showcase your pet-loving nature and walking/pet care service. Describe yourself and let potential dog owners get to know you. You should also upload a picture of yourself and several of you with some furry companions to show how much you love animals.

- Make sure to include some information about yourself like, "Hi, my name is Joe. I am 14 years old and I love taking care of my family's black lab, Buddy. I have been taking care of Buddy and taking him on walks for several years. I would love to share my love for animals with you and your family by being hired to walk your dog."

- Optimize your website to local search results. This Search Engine Optimization (SEO) can be time consuming, but it guarantees that your website will be shown higher in the organic search results when someone searches for your targeted keywords.

Method 2

Using Print Sources to Advertise

1. Call your local newspaper. Ask for the "classifieds" advertising department and place a classified

ad in the services advertising section of the newspaper. Depending on how much money you want to spend on your ad, you can have a large or a small ad; however, the key component to attracting customers is to make your ad short, concise, and catchy in order to grab the attention of potential customers.

- A good example of a successful ad would be, "Have a dog? Need your dog walked? Call xxx-xxxx for fast, reliable, low-cost dog walking services."

- Run the ad for at least a few months. This is the length of time it usually takes to attract customers.

- Depending on how large your newspaper ad is, the cost could get very expensive. However, if you choose a small ad size, you can probably spend less than $40 – depending on how widely distributed your newspaper is.

- Switch your ads every couple of weeks. Run varying ads to attract different customers. Check to see when there is a correlation between ads and customers.

- Once you determine which ad is more successful at attracting customers, use the remaining time you have left for the newspaper ad to post this particular ad.

2. Use your computer to create a flyer. Make a hand-bill or flyer as an ad that you will post, hand-out, and place around town. This is a great way to increase visibility and get new clients.

- Include your name, your phone number or email address, and a brief introduction. You could even include a picture of yourself walking a dog.

- Make different sized ads. Use bright colored paper to catch the attention of onlookers.

- You can also create simple tear-off flyers that include your advertisement at the top, with your phone number on little strips at the bottom that people can rip off to take home with them.

3. Post your flyers around town. You can create small flyers and hang ads on street-light poles facing traffic. You can also post these ads on the windshield wiper blades of cars in parking lots, though this is intrusive and not allowed everywhere. In order to reach your target customer base, it might be a good idea to visit pet store parking lots and veterinarian offices.

- Go inside these places of business and ask if they have a bulletin board for professional services. Place one of your ads on this bulletin board.

- Keep in mind that not all places will allow you to post flyers. So be careful not to break any rules by checking ahead of time.

- Try posting flyers near the mailboxes at apartment residences.

Method 3

Using Word of Mouth to Advertise

1. Ask your parents to put the word out. Your parents can be a great asset for you in advertising your dog walking business. Ask them to tell their friends, colleagues, and acquaintances that you are trying to make money by walking dogs so that they can see if anyone is interested.

- Ask your parents to say something like, "My daughter has started a dog walking business. I know that your family has a dog. Would you be interested in hiring her to walk your pet a few times a week?"

- Your parents probably have a much bigger network than you have of people they know, so this is a great situation for you to take advantage of.

- You should also ask other family members if they need their dog walked or if they know of anyone who might be interested in your dog walking services.

2. Tell your friends. Ask your friends if they would be interested in hiring you to walk their dog. Maybe their family or someone they know has a dog that needs walking too.

- Working for your friends can be complicated sometimes, so make sure you establish clear guidelines about what you both expect from the situation – how much money they will pay you and how long or how frequently you will walk the dog.

3. Let your community know. There are people you interact with every day who would benefit from your services as a dog walker. You need to find them and let them know you are available. Network within your existing community because people are usually more willing to hire people they already know and trust.

- This means talking to your teachers at school, members of your church, your neighbors, or even family friends.

4. Ask your veterinarian to recommend you. If you have a good relationship with your pet's veterinarian (or a family friend who is a veterinarian), ask them to recommend you to their clients. This would be a great (and safer) way to get the word out to fellow pet owners.

- You could even ask if you could hang one of your flyers in the vet's office.

How to become a Professional Dog Walker

Walking dogs for a living is more than just pulling on a leash and getting some exercise. You need to be a dog-lover who is in tune with the canine ways and ready to run a business. Yet, it can be a rewarding job for a dedicated person who is well-organized, professional and human and furry client-oriented. Here are some suggestions on how to start your professional dog walking career.

Part 1

Getting your Foot in the Door

1. Start dog walking or pet sitting for friends and neighbors. Apart from it being a fantastic way to make some extra cash, you're resume building, too! Ask those in your neighborhood or family friends at even the slightest mention of a vacation or being too busy to walk the dog. And when you do it once successfully, you'll likely be asked to do it again.

- Mention to your new network that you're considering making this a career, so if they could drop any of their other soon-to-be-departing or dog-owning friends of your interest, that'd be great! Right now is the time for shameless advertisement. In time, you won't have to do it at all.

- This stage is all about building up a reputation. Whatever you do, don't risk damaging it by abusing your powers. Having the key to someone's home is a serious gesture of trust -- be as responsible to your new clients as you would yourself, your grandma, or the President. That means no throwing parties, no forgetting to feed the dog, and no raiding the refrigerator (unless they allow it, of course).

2. Consider joining an agency. Point blank, the easiest way to start making money walking dogs is to join an agency. Sure, they'll take a cut of the money that's charged, but you'll get experience and they'll handle the legal mumbo jumbo. Whether the agency is for pet sitting or walking, join. It's a simple Google search away.

- The only downfall of this is that you're not your own boss. Relax -- that can come with time. But right now you're meeting people, networking, learning the ropes, and getting a feel for the dog walking market, not to mention beefing up your resume.

- Joining an agency is not an absolute, 100% must-do. You can get around it by building up your dog-walking network yourself. However, it's a lot easier to get experience and clients (and meet other people with acumen in the dog-walking business) if you join an agency.

3. Consider licensure or certification. Obtaining a dog handling certification would build some

serious credibility with clients. Some schools, such as the Canine Club Academy, offer full-tuition scholarships. And the best agencies may even require you to obtain it, either before becoming a full-time employee or after hiring.

- Certain academies, like DogTec, will help you in starting your own business too (if that interests you) in addition to dog handling and protocol. Their classes last 4 days and are in locations all across the US and British Columbia.

4. Know the ins and outs of your city. First off, you've gotta know what your city's laws are when it comes to canines *and* their walkers. Some cities require dog walkers to be insured; if you're working with an agency, hopefully they took care of that for you. But if you're thinking about doing it on your own time, it's something not to be taken lightly.

- Get to know your city's layout, too. The less you're driving around wasting money on gas, the better. Know the parks, the hidden hideaway spots, the dog parks, and back trails you can frolic with your new furry friend. You want to spend as little time commuting and as much time "working" as possible.

5. Get in good with your human clients. It may seem like dog walking is the perfect career for a surefire introvert, but the humans are where your bread and butter is. Make small chat with the doormen, the guy who works from home, and your coworkers and bosses. The better rep you have, the more professional contacts you'll have in the future.

- In addition, realize that your human clients will have all sorts of expectations, based on their own beliefs in dog-care and often with a dose of guilt that they can't spare the time to do what you are doing for them. Be generous in your compassion for their concerns (after all, they know their own pooch best) and be tolerant of the more difficult requests. Gentle persuasion and negotiation will often win the human client over!

6. Love and understand your canine clients. You need to love dogs to have a successful career with dogs. It is as simple as that. Dogs sense non-dog people and it won't be smooth riding if you aren't truly comfortable around them. There are some important considerations to think about:

- Do you know as much as possible about dogs? Know as much as you can, not just from your own experience with them but also from reading and speaking to the owners and to your local vet.

- How many dogs will you walk at any one time? Some dog-walkers can walk as many as ten dogs at once, all shapes and sizes. Consider whether you think this is a good thing or even achievable for you!

- Do you know which breeds of dogs might not be compatible or will be compatible with one another? Know this before teaming them up for a walk.

- Do you know what to do if a dog is in heat? It'll attract more than its fair share of attention and you'll need to be prepared.

- Do you know how to handle a dog that suddenly turns aggressive on you? Or on passers-by around you?

- Do you know how to poop-scoop? Do you know the local by-laws on walking dogs in certain areas etc? Read up! Your being well-informed will impress clients and will reassure them that you are not amateur and will help them to feel you are going to have their dog's best interests at heart.

7. Be able to withstand the not-so-glamourous side of dog walking. While it may sound like a dream come true (and it very well could be), not all dog walking is a glitzy, paid way to gallivant the sidewalks. You'll be dealing with poo in its very literal sense, in addition to ornery owners, ornery dogs, and ornery pedestrians. Are you ready?

- You'll also need to consider your climate. If this is going to be your main source of income, can you dog walk in the winter months? How do you feel about rain? If you're ready to tackle the less than stellar climes, be prepared! Boots, rain jacket, snow gear -- and maybe some for the pooch, too.

8. Get in shape. Being relatively fit is obviously a necessity to dog walking for a living. If you find that you get tired after a dog or two, use your free time to get in shape. Adding cardio (swimming, walking, tennis) to your list of activities will make the hours spent trotting along with Fido much more enjoyable.

- Get a good pair of shoes. When you're on the job, you'll probably be on your feet for hours on end. You don't have to go running triathlons to get accustomed to it, but it is a good idea to get a nice pair of shoes so you don't go home every night crawling on all fours like Frou-Frou over here. A decent pair will make the new physical stressors much more manageable.

Part 2

Starting your own Business

1. Consider how large you want your dog walking career to be. Be realistic - you'll probably need to start small, and allow yourself time to grow. Do you want it to be a part time or a full-time career? How much time can you devote to dog-walking? If you are young and want to make money by dog walking, make flyers and offer around your neighborhood, or put up notices on notice boards or in shop windows. For example, consider these scenarios:

- If you are a student who needs income during studies, you will have crunch times around exams and essay due dates but you will likely be fairly flexible during the rest of the time. Be honest with a potential client and explain your availability, including the possibility that there may be certain times when you will be very busy and may need to reschedule temporarily at such times. Always let them know you'll make up for it during vacation etc.

- If you want to start a permanent business, consider whether it is something you want to work 9 - 5 (or extended hours) 5 - 7 days a week, or is it something that only interests you part-time, say 2 - 3 days a week of a few hours here and there? These are important considerations that will either expand or limit your options and availability. More hours means more clients and a likelihood of referrals. Less hours will mean more devotion to a small corps of clients and a need to make it clear to them that your availability is limited to them.

2. Learn how to start a small business. If you have no business past, it's more than just a good idea

to take some classes and get your feet wet. Enlist the help of others that have a good grasp on the endeavor, can get you through the red tape, and form a solid business plan. If you want a large business, are you prepared to manage employees and cover a larger part of the city than you could do alone? Instead of just you, you'll be taking care of an entire team. You will need to:

- Get insurance and become bonded.

- Interview pet sitters, check them for reliability, train them and pay them.

- Be able to trust them to do their dog-walking according to your instructions.

- Keep good financial records, manage a payroll system, pay taxes on business income, and manage other worker's requirements.

- Keep a tight leash (no pun intended) on the client arrangements. As owner of the business, you should make all arrangements for dog-walking directly with clients and then provide the instructions, keys etc. to your employees. That way, if things don't work out with your dog-walker employee, you keep the client and substitute with a new employee.

3. Set the amount you want to charge. How you price your services will depend on the quality of your service and the length of time you have been dog-walking professionally. It will be difficult to charge higher amounts until word-of-mouth begins to boost your business and you have solid references.

- Research the field first. What are other dog-walkers charging in your area? Ask them if they are willing to divulge information to a potential competitor. Compete fairly with them - you could undercut slightly at first to get a toehold in the business. Don't undercut viciously; after all, you want to stay in this industry, not be cold-shouldered by your fellow dog-walkers. If there is no one competing, then use the internet to get some idea of the costs for your region.

- Don't under-charge or over-charge. Undercharging will lead some to think you are an amateur, perhaps even the local school kids looking for odd jobs. Charge a fair amount in return for good, reliable and professional services.

4. Print some stylish business cards. Make sure that they present a professional image and provide your contact details. Include a few short, pithy lines or words about what you offer as part of the dog-walking service. For instance:

- Say where the dogs will be walked - for example, to the parks, on green grass, in quieter areas of the city - whatever you think dog-owners would appreciate and trust.

- Explain what you will do with the dogs to keep them entertained and well-exercised - for example, that you are prepared to run with the dogs for exercise, that you will play ball/tug rope/fetch with the dogs etc.

- The ways in which you will pay attention to nutritional and medical requirements of your canine charges.

5. Advertise. Pass around flyers or business cards to let people know about your business. Stop residents walking their dogs as you walk around, introduce yourself and offer your business card to them. Begin to network with family and friends regarding your business. Start small and let your good business spread by word-of-mouth.

- There is no harm in asking your first set of clients to refer you to their friends, colleagues, etc. If they are happy with your work, many will be happy to do this. If you've built up relationships with people from past clients (security guards, doormen, maids), they may be a potential hot bed of business, too.

- Bid on keywords on Google's Adwords program, and purchase paid directory listings on dog walker directories and other websites. Hit up Craigslist, Facebook, and even veterinary bulletin boards.

6. Get a good website. The internet is increasingly becoming people's first port of call and aids them in their decision making. When choosing your domain name keep it simple by choosing a domain with relevant keywords (so your website appears on the first page of Google).

- Consider the layout and design. First impressions count and if your website is a reflection upon your service it should depict your core values (such as friendliness and professionalism) and what you have to offer. Enhance it with images or even a video so people can get a real feel for you and your service.

- Consider a website that allows users to book a time slot and services online. Some customers prefer to book online rather than over the phone.

  - If you don't know the first thing about making a website, odds are you know half a dozen people who do. So ask!

Part 3

Going the Extra Mile

1. Provide your (prospective) clients with informative resources. People looking for dog walkers have often just gotten a puppy and are looking for tips on training. New dog owners are also

interested in learning about dog health, local parks, and pet organizations. If you can be a vital source of information (cue Lori Beth Denberg) for them, they'll likely keep you around.

- Join a professional organization or two that can keep you on the up-and-up when it comes to doggy care. The International Association of Canine Professionals and the National Association of Professional Pet Sitters are two good places to start. When they ask where you learned that tidbit of info from, you just respond, "Oh, you know. I've been a member of IACP for a while now."

2. Consider value-adding with other services. It might be worthwhile adding other dog-services to your skill set. While these additional services will also add costs and some may even require business or home-office style space, if you are seriously considering making an entire career from dogs and their care, this may be the key to a lucrative career. Consider extra services such as:

- Dog-bathing and dog-grooming

- Dog-sitting (either on client's premises or at yours if you have space for boarding kennels)

- Dog-training and/or dog-listening (if you are properly qualified only)

- Spending extra time after the walk at client's home with a dog to simply be with it, play with it, feed it etc; and

- Dog medical attention - some owners can't stay home from work to medicate their dogs; you could be the answer.

3. Learn some basic dog first-aid. Ask at a local veterinary clinic for some training in basic dog first-

aid (expect to pay the vet for this advice). It will help you to fix some of the little problems that you may encounter. And while you're at this, do you know the first-aid for a dog bite?

- Your local Humane Society may be another resource you can tap into. If a veterinarian seems a bit hard to get work in with, the staff here may be a useful alternative. And you could help out pups that need love.

Dog Daycare

Dogs running in the yard at a dog daycare.

Dog Daycare, often known as "Doggy Daycare," refers to a short-term daytime care for dogs. It shares many similarities with a regular daycare for children, with the exception being that a dog daycare is for canines. It fills a niche between multi-day kennel boarding and pet sitting, where the sitter comes to the pet's home. The two share the same philosophy. Parents, or in the case of the dog daycare, owners, have a busy schedule and the often prolonged hours at work drastically reduce the time that could be spent with their children or pets.

Background

The popularity of such establishments in the United States and elsewhere has grown greatly since the early 1990s, and arose out of the more traditional kennel industry. Prior to World War II, dogs more commonly lived outside in the United States, but as urbanization spread dogs started to live indoors more frequently. Other factors, including an increase in the population of adults without children, have gradually led to more attention and money being spent on pets. The first modern dog day care in New York City, Yuppie Puppy Pet Care, Inc. was reportedly opened in 1987, by Joseph S. Sporn. San Francisco, another wealthy American city, has also been credited for spurring the dog day care trend.

Environments

There are multiple environments and varieties of dog daycare service. For example, some facilities provide a cage-free environment where dogs play under the supervision of a trained staff member.

Other facilities may provide a cage free environment for dogs to play for a portion of the day, placing dogs in cages at other times of the day. A daycare kennel is a type of facility that offers cages or runs where the dog will be placed alone during the day.

Some facilities allow dogs to play in an outside environment. Others have indoor-only facilities, where dog interact and play in an indoor area and relieve themselves in designated inside areas.

How to Care for Dogs

Are you considering bringing a dog into your home? Dogs are loyal and loving friends and usually give us back way more than we give them; however, they do require a lot of care to stay healthy and happy. If you are planning on bringing a dog into your home, there are many things to consider to ensure a long and healthy friendship.

Part 1

Preparing before you get a Dog

1. Dog-proof your house. While many objects may seem harmless to your dog or you don't expect them to be interested in them, it is best to keep small objects and human toys off of the floor or any reachable areas where your dog will be spending time.

- There are many products in your house and yard that are dangerous to dogs and should be kept well out of reach by locking them in a storage area or putting them somewhere the dog doesn't have access to. Some of the more common ones include, household cleaners, insecticides, fertilizers, and mouse and rat poisons.

- Both house plants and plants in your yard or garden can be toxic, including rhododendrons, chrysanthemum, and oleander. Identify the plants in your home and garden and then contact your veterinarian or look online at sites such as the ASPCA and Pet poison helpline for complete lists of pet toxins.

- Also, medicines both human and animal, can be toxic to your dog, especially if consumed in large amounts. Some of the foods that we eat, including chocolate, onions, raisins and grapes, and even sugarless chewing gums, can be toxic to dogs as well and should be kept well out of reach.

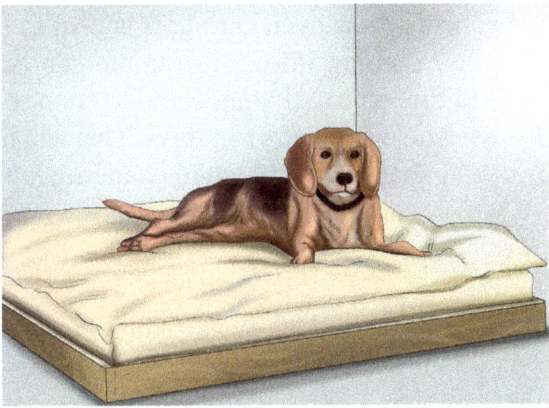

2. Give your dog a designated area. Before you bring your dog home one of the first things to decide on is where your dog will be spending their time. Think about what areas of the house they will be allowed to access and what areas you want to keep off limits. These rules should be enforced from the very beginning to avoid confusion.

- Your dog will need designated areas to eat and sleep and plenty of space to play and exercise. Initially you may want to limit the areas the dog has access to so that you can watch them closely until you get to know them and their behavior better.

- The kitchen or another area that is convenient to clean is a good place to set up food and water bowls. Once you decide on a place, you will want to keep them there at all times.

- Next decide where your dog will sleep. Some people like to have their dog sleep in the bed with them, while others prefer to get a doggie bed or crate for them to sleep separately. Be aware that once a dog is allowed to sleep in your bed it can be much more difficult to get them to sleep in their own.

- The size and activity level of your dog will determine the space needed for play and exercise. Usually, the larger the dog, the more space they will need.

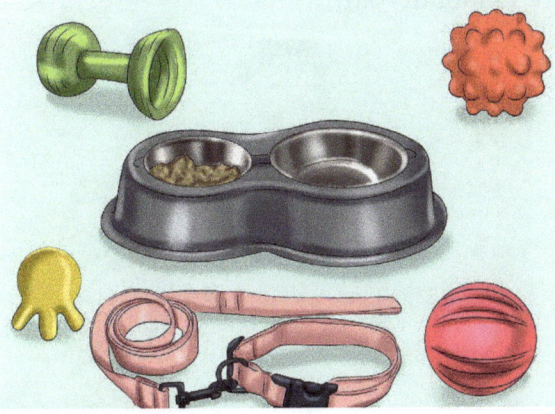

3. Purchase all the supplies you will need. Your dog may come with some of these things, but you

will need a collar and a leash that are appropriate for your dog's size, and a toy or two for starters. You will also need a food and water bowl, as well as food.

- If you know what food your dog has been eating, it is best to continue feeding them that same food, at least initially. Coming into a new home can be stressful for any dog and changing foods may add to this stress. If you decide to change foods later you can, but be sure to do so gradually over the course of 5 to 7 days. This will help to avoid problems such as diarrhea or tummy upsets that can occur when changing foods too quickly.

Part 2

Meeting your Dog's Basic Needs

1. Purchase a brand of food with high quality ingredients. You could also make your own dog food. Don't feed your dog too much sugar, fried food, or other treats for people. These will harm your dog's health over time. NEVER feed a dog chocolate.

- Generally, large breed dogs should be fed a large breed puppy formula until they are around one year of age. They then should be transitioned to an adult diet until changing to a senior diet at around six years of age. Small and medium breeds should be fed puppy formula until around one year of age when they should be changed to an adult diet.

- If a young dog becomes overweight it is fine to switch them to adult food (which is less calorific) before they are 12 months old.

2. Feed your dog on a regular schedule. Different dogs have different needs when it comes to food.

If your dog is under one year old, he or she may need several meals a day. This can be reduced to twice a day for most dogs when they are around six months old. It is normal for some dogs as they get older and usually less active, to only want to eat once a day.

- Try to feed your dog at the same times every day. This helps your dog to know when mealtime is and helps you to know how much your dog is eating. This can be important if you are trying to housebreak a dog, if a decrease in appetite occurs, and also in preventing obesity.

3. Monitor your dog's appetite and eating habits. The appropriate amount of food should be measured out to allow you to gauge how much your dog is eating. Allow your dog to eat for about 10 – 15 minutes and then the bowl should be picked up until the next feeding time. If they don't eat all of the food at this time they will be hungrier and more likely to finish it at their next feeding.

- A good way to tell if your dog is getting enough or too much food is to monitor their weight and appearance. While for some more active breeds with certain body types, seeing their ribs can be normal, for most dogs that is a sign that they are not getting enough to eat. Also, if you can't feel their ribs then they may be getting too much to eat. Always check with your veterinarian if there is a question about what your dog should weigh or look like.

- Free feeding, which is having food always available, can be an easy way to feed; however, it is discouraged. The good eater is liable to gain weight, and the fussy eater doesn't get the excitement of mealtimes. Try to stick to feeding your dog on a regular schedule.

- Puppies that are becoming overweight may need adjustments to their feeding amounts and exercise routines. It is best to consult with your veterinarian before making any changes.

- Dogs should be switched to a senior diet at around eight years of age. This helps to prevent excessive calorie intake and weight gain that can occur in an older, less active dog. It is essential to always have fresh water available at all times.

4. Provide water at all times. Keeping your dog's water bowl full of fresh water is essential. Dogs need to be able to drink when they're thirsty, and there's no harm in them drinking as much water as they want. You can put a few ice cubes in the water to keep it nice and cold when it's hot outside.

5. Make sure your dog gets plenty of exercise. Dogs need to be able to run around and play to stay healthy and happy. In general, take your dog for at least one, 30 minute, walk a day, although this may not be near enough activity for a high energy dog.

- Simply taking your dog outside to relieve itself isn't enough exercise. Make sure the dog gets tired out a bit every single day.

- The amount of exercise your dog needs will depend on their age, breed, health, and overall level of energy. Younger, very energetic breeds will require much more exercise than older, less active ones. Keep in mind that some breeds are not suited to as much exercise as others.

- If you can, find a place where it's legal to remove the leash and let him run around and stretch.

- To avoid damaging developing bones and joints in puppies, it is generally recommended to not take them running or do other repetitive high impact type of exercises, such as jumping from high places. As always ask your veterinarian for exercise recommendations.

- Interacting with your dog by playing a variety of games will keep your dog stimulated both physically and mentally while also helping to build a strong bond between the two of you.

- Also depending on your dog's activity level and your schedule, doggie day care can be a great way to give your dog the exercise they need while allowing them to interact with other dogs and people.

- Insufficient exercise can lead to boredom, which can cause many behavior issues including destructive ones. It can also lead to obesity, which can cause many related health issues and should be avoided at all costs.

- As well as exercise, mental stimulation is vital for a healthy dog. Consider playing games daily, training, and using puzzle feeders, as ways of preventing boredom.

Part 3

Keeping your Dog Healthy

1. Groom your dog. Different dog breeds require different grooming strategies. As a whole, dogs should be brushed once a week or so to help them shed hair. Long haired breeds may need more frequent brushing to avoid developing tangles and also may require regular trims. Some breeds get hot in the summer and feel better when they're shaved as it starts getting warm outside. Determine what grooming habits are best for your dog's fur and nails.

- Check for fleas and ticks while you groom, and remove them with a flea and tick comb. A quality flea prevention medication from your Veterinarian may be needed.

2. Bathe your dog every couple of weeks. Dogs don't need baths nearly as often as humans, but when they start to smell or get into mud and other messes, it's necessary to give them baths. Try to use lukewarm water and a natural, gentle shampoo that is made specifically for dogs and that will not irritate their skin.

- Dogs like to run around after a bath, so you might want to time the bath so that the dog can run around outside afterward.

- Bathing and grooming is also a good way to make sure you notice if your dog has a cut or bump that needs medical attention.

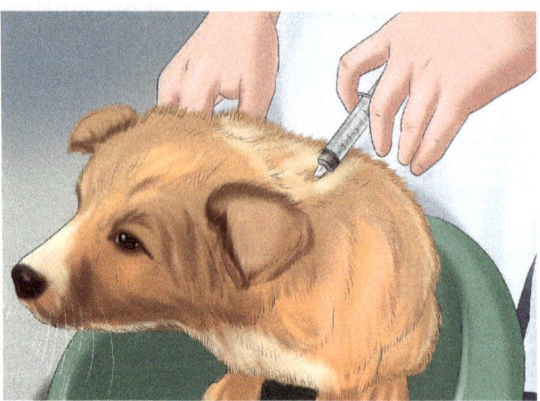

3. Make sure your dog has routine veterinary care. Regular veterinary check-ups can help prevent or detect problems early. Routine vet visits include a physical exam, fecal check, and a heartworm test. Your vet may also recommend routine blood work to check for underlying issues that haven't surfaced yet and are best treated as early as possible.

- Common regular medications that your vet may recommend include, heartworm preventative, regular dewormings, and flea and tick preventative depending on the season and what area of the country you live in.

- Make sure that your dog has had all of their necessary immunizations. This will help to keep them happy and healthy. The standard immunizations for dogs include Rabies, which is administered at 12 weeks of age or older and then every 1 to 3 years depending on your local laws and your vets recommendations. Distemper, Parvovirus, and Hepatitis are usually administered together. Puppies should receive a set of four injections every three weeks starting at six weeks of age and then annually, as adults, again based on your Veterinarian's recommendations.

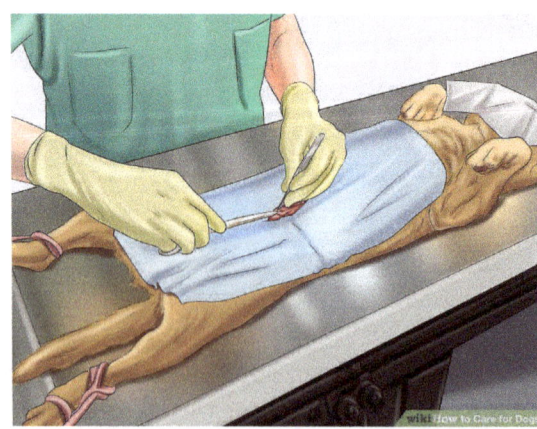

4. Consider getting your dog spayed or neutered. Spaying and neutering are procedures that

prevent unwanted pregnancies and can help to eliminate many health and behavioral issues. Neutering can prevent testicular cancers, prostate problems, urinary marking, and some aggressive behaviors in males. Spayed females have a greatly reduced incidence of mammary tumors and no possibility of uterine infections or uterine cancer.

- Ideally a puppy should have this done at around six months of age. Discuss this procedure with your veterinarian during your regular puppy visits or at the first visit after adopting an adult dog.

5. Monitor your dog's general health. Knowing your dog's normal eating habits, activity levels, and weight will help you to recognize when things change and are easy ways to track their health. Monitoring regular potty habits will help you to notice any changes that can indicate health issues. Regularly checking your dog's mouth, teeth, eyes, and ears will help to identify problems as soon as possible. You should check for lumps and cuts regularly. You should observe for any changes in the way your dog walks or moves.

- Consult your Veterinarian when you notice any changes in your dog's normal condition.

Part 4

Training your Dog

1. House train your dog. When bringing a new puppy or adult dog into your house, one of the first

things to accomplish is teaching them to relieve themselves outside, instead of indoors. Dogs of any age can be trained with the proper guidance.

- Until trained, there are a few rules to follow that will help with the process. Limit the areas your dog has access to so that they can be watched closely for signs that they are about to go and can be immediately taken out. Establish a schedule for taking them out that includes, first thing in the morning, after meal times, anytime you come home, and just before bedtime.

- Puppies will need to go out more frequently when younger and as a rule can hold their urine for an hour for every month old that they are.

- Keeping your dog on a leash, even when indoors, will allow you to monitor them more closely until they are trained. Also, when taking them outside, keep them on a leash so you can teach them to go in a specific location and to be sure that you know when they have gone.

- You can use a word such as "go" to teach them to go in a specific location. If you catch them starting to go inside, tell them "no", take them outside, and tell them to "go". Always praise them when they go where they should.

- If they have an accident in the house, be sure to clean the area thoroughly to help prevent them from wanting to go in the same place again.

- Never spank or scold a dog for going inside. The dog will only learn to fear you.

2. Crate train your dog. This will give your dog a place where they feel safe and content when you are not home and this is another popular option to prevent accidents.

- With this method, try to make the crate a fun place by giving a treat or toy and limit the amount of time that they spend in the crate to less than 4 hours at any one time, much less for younger puppies. When taking them out of the crate, immediately take them outside to their spot and don't forget to praise them when they go.

3. Teach your dog to play nicely. Dogs are generally good natured and most play well with children. Still, some like to bite and scratch a little too hard while they play, so it's important to train them how to play nicely. Reward your dog for playing gently and ignore it when it starts to bite. Eventually he or she will learn that it's more fun to be gentle.

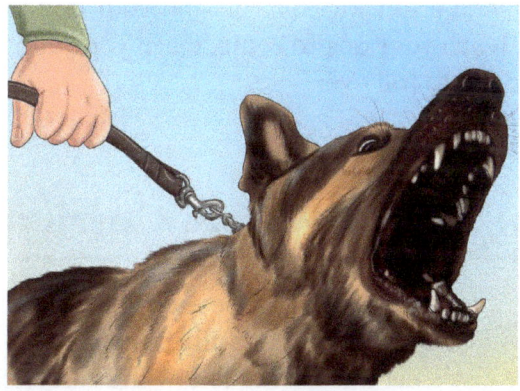

4. Teach your dog not to bark too much. Barking is a normal activity for dogs and is one form of their communication, but too much barking is a common and annoying action that many dog owners want to correct. There are many different types of barking and some require very specific actions to try to curb the problem. This is usually a slow and gradual process that also requires a lot of patience.

- There are some general guidelines for teaching your dog not to bark at every little thing. Identifying factors that cause them to bark and then eliminating them, such as closing the blinds or putting them in an area where they can't see what they are barking at is a good first step. When they don't stop barking, place them in a quiet room or their crate, with no stimulation, and allow them to calm down. Reward them as soon as they stop.

- A natural instinct is to yell at your dog for barking, but that can make them think that you are barking with them.

- If your dog is a compulsive barker, try increasing exercise and play times.

- Dogs that bark for attention should be ignored and never rewarded until the barking stops.

- This can be a difficult issue to correct and may require the help of a trained behaviorist or trainer. Bark collars should only be used after consulting with a trained professional.

5. Teach your dog a few commands and tricks. Basic commands, such as sit, stay, and come are a helpful ways to keep your dog safe by helping to prevent them from straying too far and getting lost when off leash outdoors. These also help to teach your dog their place in your relationship and to help them to bond more firmly with you.

- Other commands provide a fun way for you and your dog to interact and play. You can teach your dog to sit, teach your dog to come, teach your dog to stay, teach your dog to lie down, and teach your dog to roll over.

How to become Friends with an Unfriendly Dog

If you encounter or own an unfriendly dog it can be a challenge to create a positive interaction. However, it is possible (with most dogs) if you carefully monitor your actions and proceed slowly. When bonding with someone else's pet it is best to follow the guidance of the owner. When interacting with your dog you want to cherish and encourage small victories, such as a quick snuggle, while not being pushy. Consulting your vet can also help you to determine if there is an underlying medical reason behind the unfriendliness.

Method 1

Interacting with an Unknown Dog

1. Get the owner's permission to approach. If the owner is present, make sure to ask if it is okay to

interact with their dog. Some dogs are being trained or are too fearful to be touched, so it is best to check first. If the dog is running unsupervised, then you must follow your judgement regarding to approach or to call an animal rescue for assistance.

- When speaking with the owner you might say, "What a cute dog! Is it alright if I pet him?"

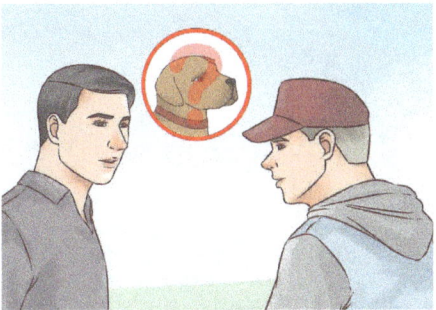

2. Explore the immediate cause of unfriendliness. When you first notice that the dog is behaving in an aggressive or standoffish way, look around you to identify possible external causes of this behavior. Are there lots of cars around which could cause anxiety? If you determine that you are the cause of the unfriendliness then you will need to approach with even more caution.

- At this point you might ask the owner (if there is one) for any tips about how to interact with their dog. They might suggest, for example, that you keep your distance for a bit.

3. Approach in an arc. When you do decide to make friendly contact (whether for the first time or after multiple interactions) avoid coming at the dog head on. This places the two of you in a confrontational position and can heighten the dog's defenses. Instead, come at the dog very slowly and slightly to the side, moving in a soft arc.

4. Keep your eyes averted. Refrain from making direct eye contact when you interact with an

unfriendly dog. Holding a dog's eyes can be seen as a dominant move and can make them withdraw from socializing with you. Instead, flick your eyes up occasionally but generally keep them elsewhere. It might help to focus on the dog's ear, for example.

5. Get on the dog's level. When you spend time with the dog try to do so at their level. Crouch down or bend down on your knees to face them. This puts you in an equal position with your potential canine friend. It lets the dog know that they have power as well, which takes away some of the pressure of these interactions and allows them to relax.

- Once you get into a crouching or seated position you lose much of your ability to retreat quickly. It is not advisable to assume this position if the dog is acting overtly aggressive.

6. Be careful when patting. Once you are in position, slowly extend a single hand out, palm up for the dog to sniff and inspect. Leave your hand hovering in air within reach of the dog's head. Do not immediately move to pet the dog. After the dog sniffs a bit you can then remove your hand and repeat the process.

- When the dog finally loosens up you can move your hand forward for a gentle pet. However, continue to avoid the facial area. This makes a dog feel vulnerable. Instead, gently rub their side or back.

- If at any point in this process the dog bares its teeth, wrinkles its nose, or growls you should retreat and try again later.

7. Go slowly. Whenever you are trying to befriend an unfriendly dog you must proceed methodically and slowly. You are on their timetable. If you try to rush the process the bond won't be as deep and the dog might retreat back into aggression or shyness.

8. Offer treats. If the dog's owner has treats then ask if you can offer a few to their pet. If the dog is running solo and you have treats, then feel free to offer them as well (with caution). It is best to give an unfriendly dog treats in an indirect way. Toss a few treats to the ground in front of the dog while looking slightly away.

- If the dog begins to associate your presence with food, then you are making progress in the battle of bonding.

9. Ignore a timid dog. Another option is to pretend that the dog is not there and go about your

business as usual. You can do this for a brief time or you can act like this over several separate interactions before you build up to an attempt at petting. If the dog sniffs you, just stand still and let it happen. It is a good sign that they are curious about you.

Method 2

Interacting with your Dog

1. Know your dog's history. Abuse or lack of socialization can help to create an unfriendly dog. It helps to gather as much information as you can about what your dog experienced in the past. This will allow you to bond with the dog while working on their trouble areas, but avoiding obvious behavioral overt triggers.

- For example, if your dog was physically abused by their previous owner (who was a man) then (if you are a man) you may face an even steeper uphill battle in building trust. Remind yourself of this and be even more patient when initiating touch with your dog.

- If your dog is only unfriendly around food, for instance, then you might want to leave it alone at these times. Try to make bonding inroads during other moments.

2. Interact in a calming environment. Some dogs are unfriendly because they are suffering

from sensory overload. To minimize this and lower everyone's stress, make your home as soothing and relaxing as possible. Keep the TV turned down low. Avoid blasting the radio. Try not to yell if you need something. Ask other members of your household to help out with this goal.

- Part of this will also push your dog's "re-set" button and signal that this is a new environment requiring new types of interactions, as compared to their previous one.

3. Be patient at all times. Your dog will likely make mistakes and these will be tests of your bond and your friendship. You must react patiently and calmly when your dog has a mishap. Offer a gentle but firm "No" and then move on.

4. Let your dog approach you first. While you are interacting in your home leave your dog alone for the most part (at least until they start to shed their unfriendliness). Expect your dog to approach you at random moments to 'check you out' by sniffing. It is best to stand still at these times and let your dog complete the inspection.

- For this to work you truly will need to stand still. Don't make a movement. Don't try to pet your dog. Don't reach out.

5. Provide positive encouragement. It is hard to be positive if your dog resists touch, but you can still be a supportive presence in their lives. Instead of offering a hug directly to them you might hug one of their toys before setting it down in front of them. Don't be afraid to use treats as well. Most dogs respond positively to small pieces of chicken or other tidbits.

- You can gently toss the treat to the floor or you can place it in your open palm for your dog to take.

6. Enjoy low-key activities. Exercise can sometimes loosen up an unfriendly dog but it can also stimulate aggression in some cases. So, use caution and stick to low-key options for the best results. Take your dog on a long walk or hike. Play Frisbee in your backyard. Just lay around and watch the sun set.

7. Participate in an obedience class. Learning new things together can bond you to your dog.

However, you must keep the stakes low and make any classes that you take a laidback event. Finding and enrolling in a local obedience class is one way to possibly change your dog's outlook. A Certified Dog Trainer can often craft unique activities that will highlight your dog's unique strengths while working on their weaknesses.

- To find a good obedience class you can check your veterinarian or you can call your local pet store. You can also look online by typing in your city's name and "obedience classes."

Method 3

Watching for Warning Signs

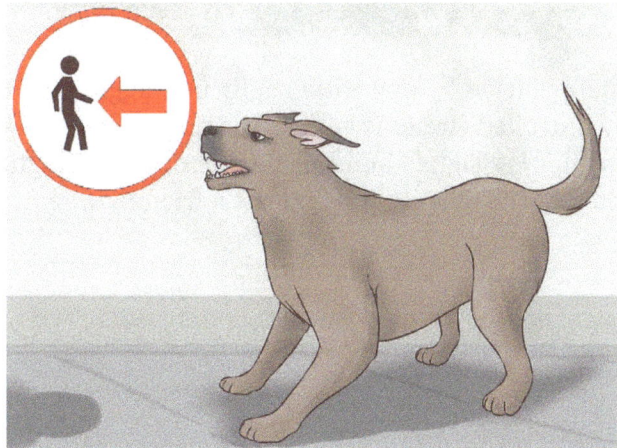

1. Pay attention to body placement. If the dog that you are interacting with starts to crouch down, as if preparing for an attack, then you need to back off immediately. Or, if the dog is behaving loosely and then stiffens suddenly it is possible that they will respond aggressively as well. Lowering their head or moving around behind you for a better angle are also negative signs.

2. Watch the teeth and eyes. A dog that is pushed beyond its limits will most likely start to growl and bare its teeth. This is a warning that often comes immediately before a biting move if left unheeded. You will also see the dog attempt to make and hold direct eye contact with you. Break this contact while keeping a close watch on the canine.

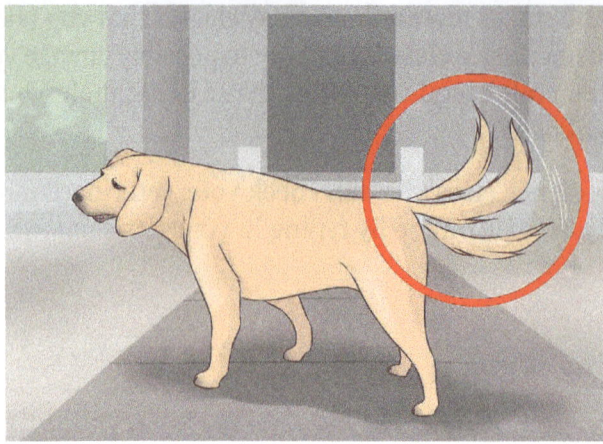

3. Look the dog's tail. A happy, friendly dog will usually be wagging his tail and wiggling overall. The tail moving in big, uncontrolled circles is generally a positive sign. If the dog starts to position their tail in a more stiff way this is a sign of building tension. The tail might still be moving or "wagging" but this is a movement borne of agitation and not a friendly wag.

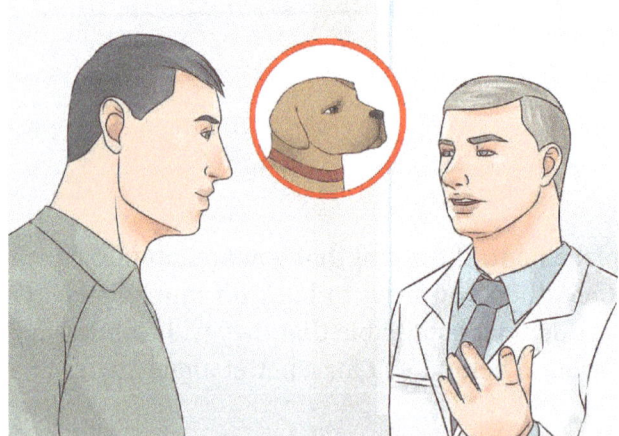

4. Consult with a veterinarian. If you've been working with your dog and just can't seem to break that bonding barrier then it may be time to talk with your vet. They can suggest some behavioral tricks that may help you. They can also look into possible medical causes for any persistent unfriendliness. Your dog may be in pain due to a seizure disorder or other condition and this could be the root cause of the problems.

- Even a change of diet has been shown to lessen the anxiety in some dogs, leading to a more positive experience for their owners.

Pet Training at Pet Day Care

Pet day care centers provide training to animals, especially dogs and cats. Being firm and providing rewards and treats are important while training pets so that they can be trained to respond to specific stimuli. This chapter elucidates crucial theories and principles of pet training.

How to give a Dog Basic Training

You don't have to be a drill sergeant to train your new companion, however training your dog takes time, love, and patience; not to mention oodles of praise. You need to be firm and consistent, but this is a time to bond with your canine companion. These are just the basic steps which will prepare you for teaching the basic and advanced commands and dealing with trouble behaviors.

Steps

1. Work with your companion regularly. Every day at first and then several times a week to keep those lessons fresh and make the exercises second nature for both of you.

2. Keep lessons and work session short enough that your pet (not to mention you yourself) doesn't get overwhelmed, frustrated, tired, or distracted. Usually 15-20 minutes is plenty.

3. Don't move on to the next set of exercises until you and your pet have mastered the present ones. And always review what has been learned before.

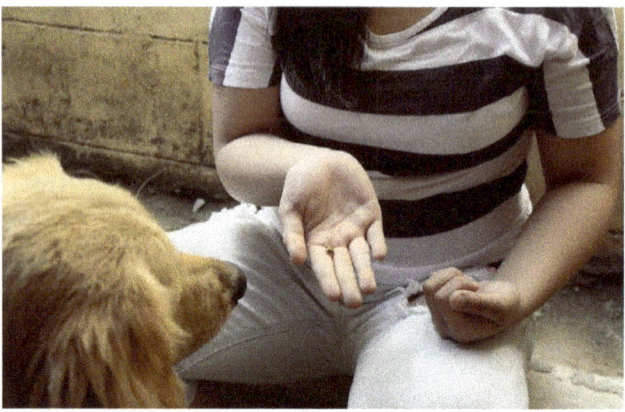

4. Have fun, but don't treat it as play time. Your pet needs to know the difference. Right after each session, make time for some type of play or attention to reward you and your pet and signify the end of the "work time".

5. Praise is your most powerful teaching technique; so use it frequently and enthusiastically! Don't hold back! Praise your dog by petting his back, rubbing his ears and head, and using a cheerful voice different from the command tone. Don't start romping with him at this point, however, or your lesson is over.

- Praise for each thing your dog does properly (even if she didn't know she was doing it or you didn't tell her to) as soon as she does it. This reinforces a pleasant result from doing the act.

- Use praise after correction only after the desired result is obtained. This will show your dog more clearly the difference in your response between her wrong behavior and the right one.

6. Correction is used stop the wrong action and show the right one. It should be done firmly, but not angrily. Praise enthusiastically when he does it right, and repeat the exercise two or three more times right away to reinforce the right action.

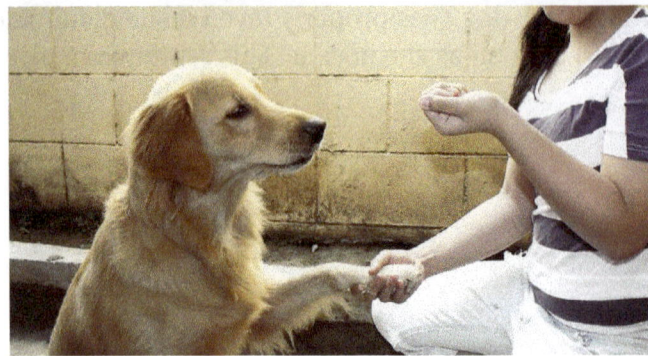

7. Use short phrases or words for commands that tell your dog what you want her to do. They need to be the same every time. Don't use similar terms to mean different things; for instance, if you use the term "down" to mean 'lie down', then use an entirely different word such as "off" to mean 'get down')

- Give commands in a firm tone of voice. At first, the command and showing her the right action should be done at the same time. Later, give the command first, and show her only if she hesitates or gets it wrong. Always follow with praise.

- Always say your dogs name before the command to alert him and make sure he is paying attention. And you should practice each of these both inside and outside, so he knows the rules apply the same way in both places.

How to Train a Dog

Are you thinking of adding a new dog to your life? Would you like your current dog to be better behaved? Would you like to train your dog to serve your needs instead being trained to serve its needs? Attending dog classes led by a professional trainer is the best approach, but not everyone can afford classes. These tips are a good start to training your canine companion. There are many philosophies and approaches to dog training, so do your research and learn what works for you and your dog.

Method 1

Preparing for Dog Training

1. Choose a dog that fits your lifestyle. After centuries of breeding, the modern dog is one of the most varied species of animal on earth. While there's probably a dog to suit every lifestyle, not all dogs will fit your specific needs. For example, if you like to relax, you should not get a Jack Russell Terrier, known for its constant barking and high energy. Instead, you might want a bulldog that would much prefer to cuddle on the couch all day. Research the personalities and care requirements of various breeds. Ask dog owners about their breed's personality.

- Since most dogs live for 10 – 15 years, getting a dog is a long-term commitment. Make sure the breed's temperament is a good match for your lifestyle.

- If you haven't yet started a family, consider whether you'll have young children around the house in the next decade. Some breeds are not recommended for households with children.

2. Don't get an aspirational dog. Be honest with yourself about the compatibility of the dog you

want with your lifestyle. Don't get a dog that needs a lot of activity just because you want a reason to jumpstart a healthier lifestyle yourself. If you can't follow through on exercising your high-energy dog, you and the dog will both end up frustrated.

- Write down the needs and temperament of the breed, as well as how you will meet those needs.

- If it's going to take significant effort to change your lifestyle, you need to choose a different dog.

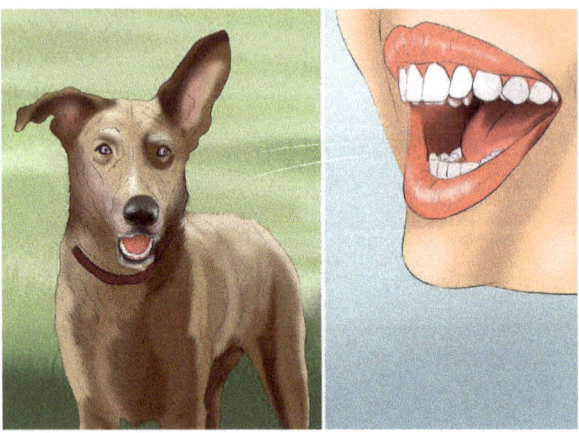

3. Give your dog a practical name. He needs to be able to learn his name easily, so you can hold his attention during training. The name should also have clear, hard sounds the dog can recognize. Names such as "Buddy" or "Rover" or "Bee Bee" have distinct sounds that stand out from the regular flood of human speech your dog hears.

- Use your dog's name often when you are playing, petting him, training him, or need to get his attention.

- If your dog looks at you when you say his name, you know he's learned it.

- Create a positive association with his name so he'll continue to focus on you when you say it. Praise him when he responds to his name, and give him treats.

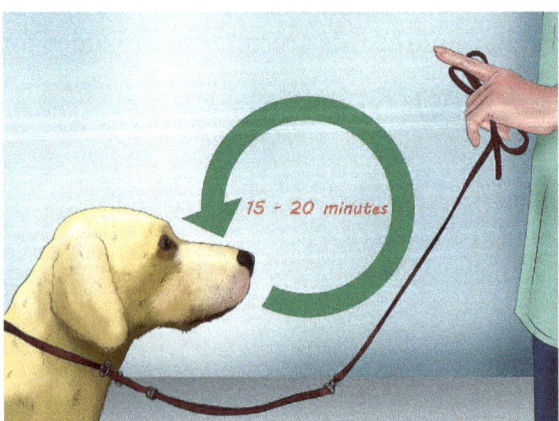

4. Schedule enough time for training. You'll need to set aside 15 – 20 minutes a couple of times

each day for formal training sessions. Puppies have a short attention span and get bored easily, just like a toddler would.

- Those sessions are not the only time you'll train your dog, though. Training actually happens throughout the day when interacting with your pet. He's learning from you every time you interact.

- Bad dog habits develop when owners let dogs get away with bad behavior outside of dedicated training sessions. So, always keep an eye on your dog outside of training sessions. If he knows it during training sessions, then make sure he remembers it outside of training.

5. Prepare your mental state for training sessions. When you're working with your dog, be calm and neutral. Any form of agitation and excitement on your part will negatively affect the outcome of training. You should be mindful of the fact that the goal of training is to be able to reinforce good dog behavior and to ignore or not reinforce bad ones. It may sound strict but producing a well trained dog requires the determination and conviction to see it through.

6. Choose the proper equipment. A 6-foot leash and flat collar or martingale collar may be all the you need to start, besides your treats. Consult a trainer for advice on other equipment like a "Promise Leader" head halter, a "No Pull" harness, a metal training collar, or other device. Puppies or small dogs generally do not need harsh equipment. Larger dogs may temporarily need specialized equipment (like the "Promise Leader") to keep their focus.

Method 2

Applying General Training Principles

1. Manage your expectations and mood. Not every training day is going to be perfect, but don't get frustrated and don't take it out on your dog. Adjust your own behavior and attitude to encourage your dog's ability and confidence to learn. If you have a calm mood, generally your dog will, too.

- If the dog becomes afraid of your bad mood, he will not learn anything new. He'll only learn to be wary and not trust you.

- Dog training classes and a good trainer can help you improve your behavior which will translate to success with your dog.

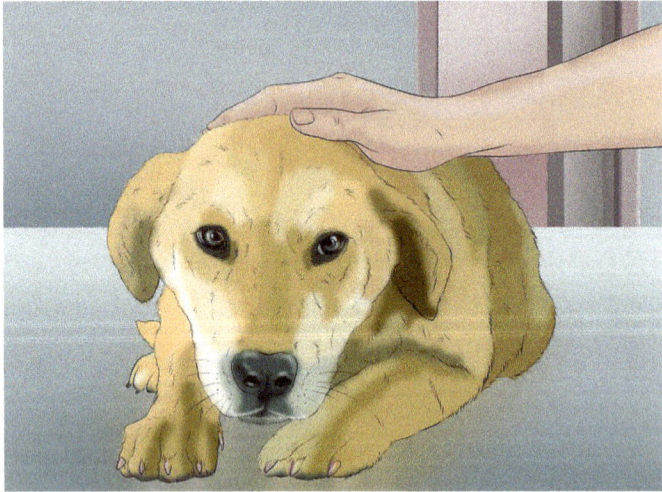

2. Keep your dog's temperament in mind. All dogs have different temperaments. Just like kids, different breeds learn differently and at different rates. Some dogs are stubborn and will challenge you at every turn. Others will bend over backwards to please you. You may need to adjust your training techniques to meet the need of your dog's temperament.

3. Give immediate rewards. Dogs don't understand long-term cause and effects. They learn fast. You must praise or reward your dog within **2 seconds** of a desired behavior to reinforce that behavior. If you wait too long, he will not associate the reward with the action you asked him to perform.

- Furthermore, you must make sure that your praise is fast enough to be accurate. Otherwise, you may reward behaviors that you don't want.

- Imagine, for example, that you are teaching your dog the "sit" command. He sits for just a moment, but by the time you praise and reward him, he's started standing back up. In this case, you are rewarding the standing behavior, not the sitting behavior.

4. Consider clicker training. Clicker training is a method of delivering immediate praise with the help of a clicker. You can click faster than you can give a treat or pet your dog's head. As such, clicker training reinforces good behavior fast enough for a dog's learning speed. It works by creating a positive association between the click sound and rewards. Eventually, your dog will consider the sound of the clicker itself reward enough for good behavior. You can apply the principle of clicker training to any dog command.

- Click the clicker device, then immediately give the dog a treat. This creates a positive association with the click sound. Later, that sound will "mark" a behavior as correct so the dog knows that he did something right.

- When the dog performs a desired behavior, make the click sound, then give him a treat. Once he's performing that behavior consistently, you can give the behavior a command name. Begin tying the command and the behavior together with the help of the clicker.

- For example, before you ever teach your dog the "sit" command, give the click sound, a treat, and praise when you find him sitting. When he begins sitting just to get the treats, start saying the word "sit" to get him into position. Pair it with the click sound to reward him. Eventually, he will learn that sitting in response to the "sit" command will earn him a click reward.

5. Be consistent. Your dog won't understand what you want from him if his environment lacks consistency. Everyone who lives with your dog should understand and be on board with his training goals. For example, if you are training your dog not to jump on people, don't let the kids allow the dog jump all over them. This will undermine all the training you've done.

- Make sure everyone uses the exact commands your dog learns in training. He doesn't speak English, and can't tell the difference between "sit" and "sit down." Using those terms interchangeably will only confuse him.

- Because he won't make a clear connection between a single command and a single action, his response to the command will be hit or miss.

6. Always reward success and good behavior with praise, and sometimes a small treat. Small treats help motivate your dog to learn his training. The treat needs to be small, tasty, and easily chewed. You don't want it to interrupt the training session or make them full too quickly.

- Consider how long it takes to chew a hard treat versus a semi-moist treat like "Bill Jack" or

"Zuke's Mini Naturals." Treats about the size of a pencil eraser head are enough to get the positive point across, and you don't have to wait long for your dog to eat it.

7. Use "high value" treats when needed. When teaching difficult or important a command, use a "high value" treat to raise the stakes for him. Examples include freeze-dried liver, roasted chicken breast chunks, or slices of turkey lunch meat.

- As the dog learns the command, phase out the high value treats and bring them back as needed to advance your training, but *always* give him praise.

8. Train on an empty stomach. Don't feed as large a meal as usual a few hours before training your dog. The more your dog wants the treat, the more focused he'll be on the task he needs to perform to get it.

9. Always end training on a positive note. Even if the training session did not go well and your dog

didn't catch on to a new command, end on something that you can praise him for. By ending the training session with a command he's already mastered, the last thing he remembers will be your love and praise.

10. Discourage barking. If your dog barks at you when you don't want him to, just ignore him until he stops, and then reward him with praise. Sometimes they bark at you for attention, while other times it may be out of frustration.

- Do not throw a ball or toy. This only teaches him that if he barks, he'll get you to do something he wants.

- Don't yell at the dog to be quiet, as this rewards him with attention.

Method 3

Teaching the "Heel"

1. Take your dog on regular walks with a leash. This is important not just for training, but for his physical and mental health. Depending on what breed of dog you have, he may need a lot of exercise to keep him happy and in shape.

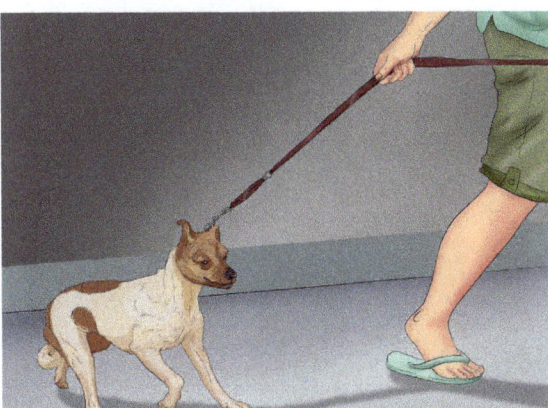

2. Discourage pulling. Most dogs will pull on the leash when they're learning to take walks. When he starts pulling, stop immediately. Don't take another step until the dog comes to your side and focuses his attention on you.

3. Change directions. An even more effective method is to walk in the opposite direction and encourage your dog to come with you. Once he's caught up, praise and treat him.

4. Make it fun to be by your side. Your dog's natural impulse is to chart his own course and investigate his environment. You need to make walking by your side more appealing that that. Use an enthusiastic voice when changing directions, and lavish him with praise when he comes back to your side.

5. Pair the behavior with a verbal command. Once the dog walks consistently at your side, you can give the behavior a name, like "heel" or "let's go."

Method 4

Teaching the "Come"

1. Understand the value of the command. The "come" is used whenever you want your dog to come to you. This command is potentially life-saving, as it can prevent your dog from running off if he gets loose.

2. Prepare your dog for "come" training. You always want to start training indoors (or in your fenced yard) with low distraction. Attach a 6-foot leash to your dog's collar so that you have a way to keep his attention and prevent him from running away.

3. Attract your dog's attention. You want to make him run toward you. You can do this with high-pitched noises associated with play, with a toy, with an excited clap, or just opening your arms. Running a short distance away from him and then stopping can also work, as dogs will naturally start to chase.

- Use praise and your "happy voice" to encourage him to move toward you.

4. Give immediate praise. Sound your clicker, give him praise in your "happy voice," and give him a treat when your dog reaches your side.

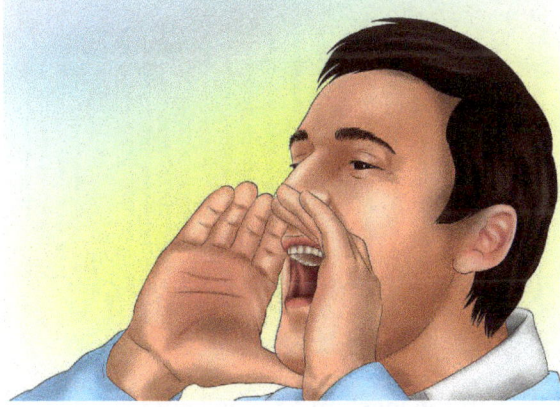

5. Pair the behavior with the verbal command. As your dog begins to realize he'll be rewarded for

coming to you, start giving the verbal command "come." When he responds to the command, reinforce it in praise by pairing it with "good": "good come!"

6. Move the training to more public spaces. Because the "come" command could save your dog's life, he must learn to respond to it even when he's distracted. Move the training sessions from your home or yard to a public park. There are more sights, sounds, and smells demanding his attention there.

7. Increase the leash length. You began training with a 6-foot leash, but you want your dog to come longer distances than that. Try attaching two leashes together to increase the distance.

8. Work up to training your dog off the leash in a fenced environment. This will teach him to come over long distances.

- Ask someone to help with off-the-leash training. You can play "ping pong" and take turns calling the dog to each of you.

9. Give enormous rewards. Because this command is so important, the praise you give for performing it should be extravagant. Responding to the "come" command should be the best part of your dog's day.

10. Do not create a negative association with this command. No matter how upset you are, never reinforce the "come" with anger. Even if you're furious that your dog slipped the leash and ran free for five whole minutes, lavish him with praise when he finally responds to the "come." Remember that *you're praising the last thing he did did*, and the last thing he did was to come to you.

- Don't ever correct, yell, yank or in any way make coming to you a bad thing. You can undo years of training with one bad experience.

- Never do something your dog won't enjoy after giving a "come." Though you may be tempted to give the command when you need to give him a bath, trim his nails, or cleans his ears, the "come" should always lead to joy.

- If you have to do something your dog won't like, just go and get the dog yourself instead of giving the command. Praise the dog along the way for being calm and accepting of the task. You can use treats, of course.

11. Go back to basics. If you have a scare where your dog runs loose and ignores the "come" command, go back to leash training. Continue working on the leash until he responds reliably to the "come."

- Don't rush the training on this command. It's too important to do half-heartedly.

12. Reinforce the training throughout your dog's life. Because this behavior is so important, it must be reinforced throughout his entire lifetime. If you take off-leash hikes with your dog, keep treats in your pocket to reinforce the command.

- You also want a command to let the dog know that it does not have to be right next to you all the time. Something like "free" is one way to phrase it, but the idea is that the dog can do what it wants and is not under command until you give it one.

13. Keep the fun going. You don't want the dog to think that every time they come to you, the fun

stops, someone puts on the leash, and they go back home. Otherwise, you will start to get less reliable and less happy "comes." So, call the dog, praise them when they arrive and set them "free" to play again.

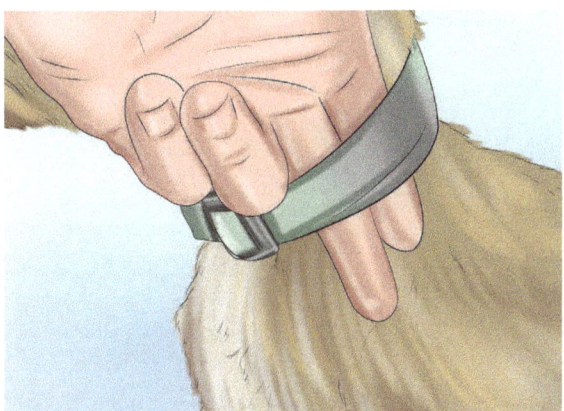

14. Acclimate the dog to collar grabs. This doesn't have to be paired with any verbal commands. When the dog comes to you, grab his collar so he doesn't grow skittish every time he feels someone touch it.

- When you lean over to reward him for the "come," include grabbing the collar in your hand and petting around the neck as you give him his treat.

- Once in a while, but not always, the leash should be attached when you grab the collar.

- Also, you can always attach a short leash and let them "free" again. Leashes should mean fun things are about to happen and we get to go places. There is no room for harsh corrections.

Method 5

Teaching the "Listen"

1. Understand the purpose of the "listen" command. Also known as the "watch me" command, the "listen" is one of the first commands you should teach your dog. You'll use it to get your dog's attention so you can give him the next command or direction. Some people just use their dog's

name instead of the "listen." This is especially useful if you have more than one dog. That way, each individual dog will know when you want it to focus on you.

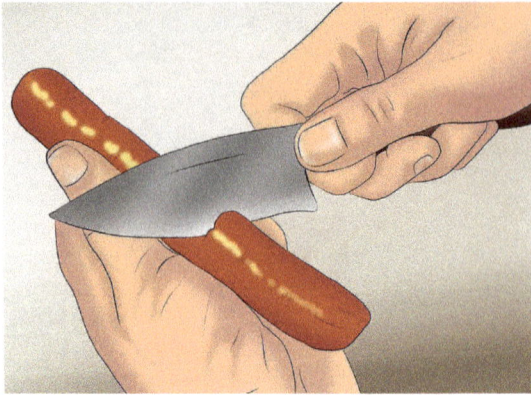

2. Prepare a handful of treats. These may be dog treats you buy at the store, or hot dogs cut into small pieces. Choose a treat that you know your dog loves and will perform for.

3. Stand near your dog. Don't engage with him, though. If he reacts to your presence, stand still and look away until he loses interest.

4. Say "Listen" in a quiet but firm voice. If you're using your dog's name instead of the "listen" or "watch me" commands, say his name instead. The tone and volume should be the same as if you were calling a person's name to get their attention.

5. Don't raise your voice to get his attention. Save the big booming voice for "life saving" situations, like if he escapes his fence or leash. If you rarely raise your voice, you'll get your dog's undivided attention when you do need to yell. But if you are always "loud" to your dog, they will ignore that sound and tune it out. Shouting will no longer be regarded as something that commands special attention.

- Dogs have excellent hearing — far better than ours. A fun twist on this command is to see how quietly you can whisper and have your dog respond. People will think you are the "dog whisperer" when you can get him to perform commands with hardly a whisper.

6. Give an immediate reward for the desired response. As soon as your dog stops what he's doing and looks toward you, praise him and give him a treat. Make the click sound before giving praise or a treat if you're using clicker training.

- Remember that your response must be *immediate*. The faster you reward him, the better he'll understand the relationship between command, behavior, and reward.

7. Discontinue treats eventually. Once he's mastered the command, you shouldn't give him treats for performing it; however, you should still use your clicker or give verbal praise.

- Weaning the dog off treats is important because he may start to expect treats all the time. You'll end up with a dog who only performs when you have food.

- Praise your dog regularly even after he's mastered a command, but treat him intermittently. That's the way to keep it solid in his doggy vocabulary.

- Once he's mastered command, you can use treats to shape the behavior to be faster or more accurate. He will soon realize that the treats come with the command or activity that follows the "listen."

Method 6

Teaching the "Sit"

1. Get your dog into a standing position. The purpose of the "sit" is get your dog to transition from standing to sitting, not just continue sitting. Walk into your dog or step away from him to get him into a standing position.

2. Position yourself in his line of sight. Stand directly in front of the dog so that his attention is focused on you. Let him see that you have a treat in your hand.

3. Focus the dog's attention on the treat. Begin with the treat held down at your side. Raise that hand in front of the dog's nose to let him get the scent, then to above his head level.

- When you hold the treat above the dog's head, most dogs will naturally sit to get a better view of it.

4. Give him an immediate treat and praise. Follow the routine of clicker-treat/praise or just treat and praise. Say "good sit" when he's performing the behavior you are practicing. He may be slow at first, but more treats and praise will speed up his response.

- Make sure that you do not praise him until his butt touches the ground. If you praise half-way through the sit, the dog will think that is what you want.

- Also, make sure that you do not praise him for getting back up, or you will get that behavior instead of the sit.

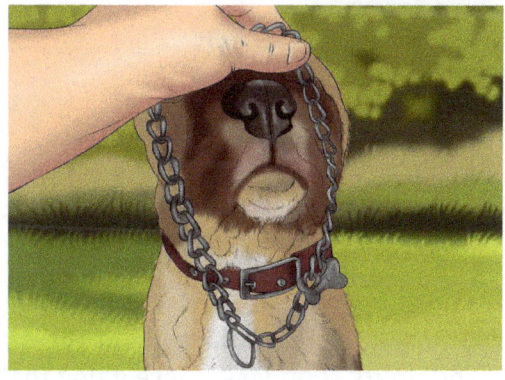

5. If your dog does not sit with the treat technique, you can use your leash and collar. Stand next

to the dog, facing the same direction as him. Place a little backward pressure on the collar to encourage a sit.

- You may even need to encourage the sit by adding a little gentle scoop behind the dog's hind legs. Gently lean the dog backward with the help of the collar while doing this.

- As soon as he sits, give him immediate praise and reward.

6. Don't repeat the command. You want the dog to respond on the first utterance, not the second, third, or fourth. If the dog does not perform the behavior within 2 seconds of your command, reinforce the command with the help of your leash.

- When you begin training a dog, never give a command that you are not in a position to reinforce. Otherwise, you risk training the dog to ignore you because there is no follow through from your end and the commands have no meaning.

- Create a positive meaning for the dog with praise and consistency.

7. Praise natural sitting behavior. Look for times throughout the day when your dog just sits on his own. Praise that behavior, and pretty soon you'll have a dog that sits for attention instead of jumping or barking at you.

Method 7

Teaching your Dog to Lie Down

1. Get your dog's attention. Get some food treats or a toy and find your dog. Hold the toy or treat in view so he focuses on you.

2. Use the treat or toy to encourage your dog to lie down. Do this by moving the toy or treat onto the ground in front of the dog, between his front legs. His head should follow it, and his body should follow shortly thereafter.

3. Give immediate praise. When the dog's stomach is on the ground, lavish him with praise and give him the treat or toy. Be accurate with your praise, too. If you praise him halfway down or up, that is the behavior you will get.

4. Increase your distance. Once he's learned the behavior with the promise of a treat below him, move a little farther away. The hand signal for "down" will become your flat hand — palm down — moving in a downward direction from in front of your waist to your side.

- As the dog gets more consistent with the "down" behavior, add a verbal "down" or "lie down" command.

- Always praise him immediately when his belly is on the ground.

- Dogs read body language well and learn hand signals quite quickly.

5. Lengthen the "down." As he gets more reliable with "down," pause a few seconds before praising and treating to encourage him to hold the position.

- If he pops up to get the treat, do not give it to him, or you will be rewarding the last behavior he did before the treat.

- Just start again, and the dog will understand that you want him all the way down on the ground, as long as you are consistent.

6. Don't lean over your dog. Once your dog has caught onto the command, stand up straight when giving it. If you loom over him, you'll have a dog that only lays down when you are leaning over him. You want to work on being able to get your dog to lie down from across the room, eventually.

Method 8

Training your Dog to "Wait" at Doorways

1. Begin doorway "wait"-training early. Teaching a dog to respect the threshold is important. You do not want a dog that runs out the door every time it opens — that could be dangerous for him. Doorway training doesn't need to happen every single time you go through a doorway. But you should make the most of your training opportunities early in your puppy's life.

2. Place the dog on a leash. You should have him on a short leash that allows you to change his direction from a close distance.

3. Walk to the door. Bring the dog along with you on his leash.

4. Give a "wait" command before stepping through. If your dog moves to follow you when you step through the door, use the leash to stop his forward movement. Try again.

5. Praise him when he waits. When he realizes that you want him to stay in the door instead of walking through it with you, lavish him with praise and rewards for the "good wait."

6. Teach him to sit in the threshold. If the door is closed, you can even teach your dog to sit as soon as you place your hand on the doorknob. He'll then wait while the door is opened, and not cross the threshold until you release him. This training should be done on leash at the beginning, for his safety.

7. Give a separate command to encourage him through the doorway. You might use a "come" or a "free." Whatever command you use, it should be the only thing that allows your dog to exit your home.

8. Increase the distance. Practice leaving the dog at the threshold and do something on the other side. You might get the mail or take out the trash before you return and praise him. The idea is that you do not always call him across the threshold to meet you. You can also come back to him.

Method 9

Teaching your Dog Positive Food Behaviors

1. Have him wait patiently while you prepare his meal. There's nothing more annoying than a dog who jumps and barks while you're trying to prepare his meal. Instead, use the "wait" command he learned in doorway training to have him wait outside the threshold of the room where he's fed.

- When you're ready, have your dog work for his food by commanding the dog "sit" and "stay" while you place the food on the ground.

- Stand up and wait a few breaths before giving your release word. You can use "free" or you can create a new command for feeding time like "get your food" or "yummy." Try to choose something you wouldn't accidentally say to other people, such as "time to eat," or, "let's eat," as this might falsely cue your dog that it's time for his dinner.

- Eventually, he will sit on his own as soon as he sees his feeding bowl.

2. Hand feed your dog. At meal time, start feeding your dog out of your hand. Then use your hands to put the rest of the food in the bowl. This will put your scent on your dog's bowl and also normalize having your hands around their bowl and food. This should help fix or prevent any food aggression tendencies.

3. Teach your dog to "leave it." Teaching your dog to move his nose away from food and other items can be beneficial in a number of situations, including when food is accidentally dropped on the floor during family dinner or when your dog seems interested in picking up something potentially harmful during a walk. To teach this command, do the following:

- Stage one: Hold a treat in your closed hand. The dog will probably lick, sniff, and paw at your hand in an attempt to get to the treat. Eventually, when the dog moves his nose away, praise him and give him the treat.

- Stage two: Add in the words "leave it." Say these words when your dog decides to move his nose away.

- Stage three: Hold one treat in your palm in front of the dog and one behind you in the other hand. Instruct your dog to "leave it." If the dog gets too close to the treat, make a fist to hide the treat and say "no" or "uh-oh" to show the dog that he won't be rewarded or noncompliance. When he obeys the "leave it" command, give him the treat that's behind your back.

- Stage four: Place the treat on the floor. Move the treat from your palm to the floor. Continue to reward your dog with the treat you have behind your back.

- Stage five: Put your dog's leash on and walk past the treat on the floor. Command him to "leave it" without jerking the leash. If he eats the treat, go back to an earlier stage.

- Stage six: Start using the "leave it" command outside of your home.

Method 10

Teaching the "Take" and "Drop It" Commands

1. Understand the command. The "take" is used whenever you want the dog to take something you offer into his mouth.

2. Give your dog a toy to play with. Give him the verbal command "take" as you do so. As he takes the toy in his mouth, reward him for the behavior with praise. (Plus, he gets to play with the toy!)

3. Transition to less rewarding objects. It's easy for a dog to learn "take" when the object is so much fun! When he's mastered the connection between command and behavior, move on to boring objects. Examples might include newspapers, light bags, or anything else you might want him to carry.

4. Pair "take" training with "drop it" training. Once he takes the toy, use the command "drop it" to have the dog release the toy back to you. Give him a treat and praise when he releases the toy, then start again with "take." You don't want the dog to think that the fun stops every time he releases the toy.

- Do not get into a tugging match with the dog. When you tug, the dog tugs back harder.

Method 11

Teaching the "Stand"

1. Understand the value of the "stand" command. The value of the "sit" and "wait" seem obvious,

but you may not understand at first why the "stand" is an important skill to teach your dog. You'll won't use the "stand" every day, but you'll need it throughout the dog's life. For example, a dog who can stay calmly in a "stand" is the ideal patient at a vet clinic or client at a groomer's.

2. Prepare for the training session. Grab his favorite toy or prepare a handful of treats to both focus your dog's attention and reward him for learning the command. Put the dog in a starting "down" or "lie down" position when working with the "stand" command. He should move from lying down to standing up to get his toy or treats.

3. Focus the dog's attention. You want to coax him into the standing position by having him follow the toy or treat. Hold the toy or treat in front of his face, at nose height.

- If he sits, thinking that will earn him a reward, try again, but with the treat or toy slightly lower.

4. Encourage the dog to follow your hand. Flatten your hand with your palm down. If you're using

a treat, hold it with your thumb against your palm. Start with your hand in front of his nose and move it away a few inches. The idea is that the dog will stand up while following your hand.

- You may need to use your other hand to encourage him from underneath his hips to get the idea at first.

5. Give immediate praise. As soon as he reaches the standing position, praise and treat. Although you haven't yet started using the verbal "stand" command, you can use it in your praise: "good stand!"

6. Add the verbal "stand" command. At first, you will work only on getting your dog to stand by following the hand that holds his toy or treat. When he's mastered that concept, begin incorporating the "stand" command into the training sessions.

7. Combine the "stand" with other commands. There are many ways to combine commands. After

getting your dog to "stand," you might add a "wait" or "stay" command if you want the dog to stand for longer periods of time. You can also follow with a "sit" or "down" to do some "doggy drills," and gradually increase the distance between you and the dog. Eventually, you'll have your dog performing these commands from across the room.

Method 12

Teaching the "Speak"

1. Understand the command. The "speak" command teaches your dog to bark in response to your verbal cue. On its own, this command is something of a novelty. But in combination with the "quiet" command, it can help manage a barking problem in an overly vocal dog.

- Take extreme caution when teaching this command. Inexperienced trainers sometimes find "speak" training spirals out of control. They end up with a dog who barks at them all the time.

2. Clicker train your dog. "Speak" training requires immediate praise, more so than other commands do. Teach your dog to associate the click sound with a treat by clicking and treating a few times in a row.

- Continue this clicker training until your dog sees the click sound as a reward in and of itself. The treat will come later.

3. Figure out when your dog barks most. This will vary from dog to dog, so you have to observe your specific pet. He might bark most reliably when you withhold a treat, when someone knocks on the door, when someone rings the doorbell, or when someone honks a horn.

4. Recreate the triggering event. Once you've figured out what makes your dog bark, perform that action in front of your dog. The idea is to encourage him to bark on his own, then praise him for the action.

- You can see how this might be dangerous in the hands of an inexperienced trainer.

- That's why "speak" training is a little different from the other commands. You'll incorporate the verbal command from the very beginning. That way, the dog doesn't think you're praising him for his natural behavior.

5. Use the verbal "speak" command from the beginning. As soon as your dog barks for the very first time, give the verbal "speak" command, click, and give him a treat.

- The other commands thus far have taught the behavior first, then added a command that preceded the behavior.

- However, "speak" training gets out of hand too easily that way. The dog gets rewarded for barking at first.

- Thus, it's better to associate the verbal command with the behavior already in progress. Never reward the dog for barking without the verbal command.

6. Combine the "speak" with the "quiet" command. If you have a dog who naturally barks too much, you might not think teaching him to "speak" is going to help your situation. However, if you teach him to "speak," then you can also teach him to "quiet." While you may not need the "speak" for a dog who barks too much, you definitely need the "quiet."

- Once your dog has mastered the "speak," begin incorporating "quiet" into your training sessions.

- Give the "speak" command.

- However, instead of rewarding the "speak" (barking), wait until the dog stops barking.

- Give the verbal "quiet" command.

- If the dog remains silent, reward the "quiet" (no barking) with a click and a treat.

Method 13

Crate Training your Dog

1. Understand the value of crate training. You might think it cruel to pen a dog up in a crate for

hours at a time. But dogs are instinctively den animals, so confined spaces are not as oppressive to them as they are to us. In fact, crate trained dogs will seek out their crates as a source of comfort.

- Crate training is a useful way to manage your dog's behavior when he's unsupervised for extended periods of time.

- For example, many owners crate their dogs when they go to sleep or leave the house.

2. Begin crate training young. Although older dogs can be taught to enjoy their crates as well, it's easier to train a young dog.

- If your puppy is a large breed, don't train him in a large crate that you think he'll grow into.

- Dogs won't relieve themselves where they sleep or relax, so you need the crate to be appropriately sized.

- If you use a crate that's too large, he might urinate in the far corner of it because he has so much space.

3. Make the crate an inviting space. Don't isolate him in the crate immediately by locking the door the first time you get him to enter it. You want him to create a positive association with the crate, so that he enjoys his time in there.

- When you begin the crate training process, place the crate somewhere the household gathers. The idea is to make the crate part of the social scene rather than a place of isolation.

- Place a soft blanket and some of your dog's favorite toys inside the crate.

4. Encourage him to enter the crate. Once you've made the crate an inviting space, use treats to lure him inside. At first, place some outside the door so he can explore the exterior of the crate. Then, place treats just inside the door, so he will poke his head in to retrieve them. As he grows more comfortable, place the treats further and further inside the crate.

- Do this until your dog enters the crate without hesitation.

- Always speak in your "happy voice" when acclimating your dog to the crate.

5. Feed the dog in his crate. Once he's comfortable entering the crate for treats, reinforce the positive association with mealtime.

- Place his dog bowl wherever he's comfortable eating. If he's still a little anxious, you might have to place it right by the door.

- As he grows more comfortable over time, place the dog bowl further back into the cage.

6. Begin closing the door behind him. With treats and feeding, you'll find that your dog is growing more acclimated to being in the crate. He still needs to learn how to cope with the door being closed.

- Begin closing the door at mealtime, when the dog too distracted by his food to notice what's going on at first.

- Close the door for very short periods, lengthening the time as the dog grows more comfortable.

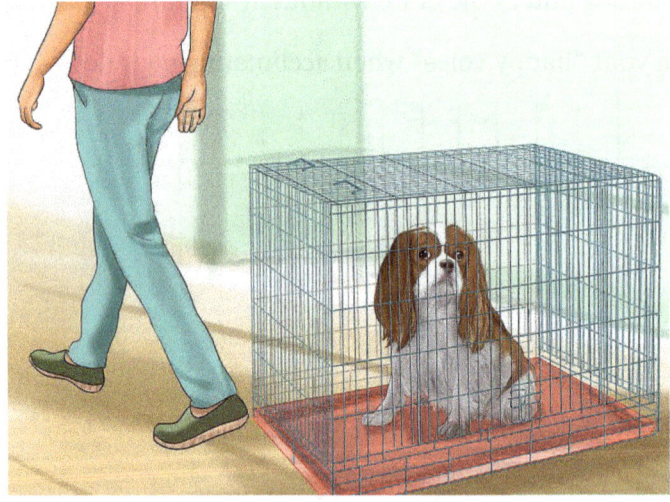

7. Don't reward the dog for whining. When a puppy whines, it may be adorable and heartbreaking, but when a grown dog whines, it can drive you nuts. If your puppy whines inconsolably, you may have left him inside the crate for too long. However, you cannot release him from the crate until the whining stops. Remember — every reward you give reinforces the dog's last behavior, which was whining in this case.

- Instead, release the dog once he's stopped whining.

- The next time you close the door on the crate, leave him in for a shorter period of time.

8. Comfort your dog during long crate sessions. If your puppy cries when he's alone in the crate, bring the crate into your bedroom at night. Have a tick tock clock or white noise machine to help the puppy get to sleep. Make sure that they have already eliminated outside and don't need to urinate or defecate.

- Young puppies should be crated in your room at night so that you can hear them tell you they need to go out in the middle of the night. Otherwise, they will be forced to mess in the crate.

How to Train a Cat

Cats are incredibly independent creatures. In fact, researchers have found that even though humans have kept cats as pets for at least 9,000 years, house cats are only semi-domesticated. Training a cat can be difficult, because it can require the trainer to convince the cat that the task at hand is a worthwhile skill to learn. But with a little patience, you can train your cat to be a better pet in more ways than one.

Method 1

Training a Cat to use a Litter Box

1. Put the litter box in a quiet location. Cats prefer to relieve themselves in a peaceful location

without a lot of action or loud noises in the background. However, cats also do not like having a litter box that is too far out of the way.

- Make sure your cat can physically access his litter box. Do not put the box on a high shelf or an otherwise difficult to reach area if your cat is old and has trouble jumping or climbing.

- Avoid noisy or high-traffic areas. Do not place a litter box next to a washing machine, for example, or in a crowded hallway that gets a lot of foot traffic. Cats want peace and privacy, but they also want convenience.

- Do not put your cat's litter box in close proximity to its food and water dishes. This may discourage your cat from using the litter box.

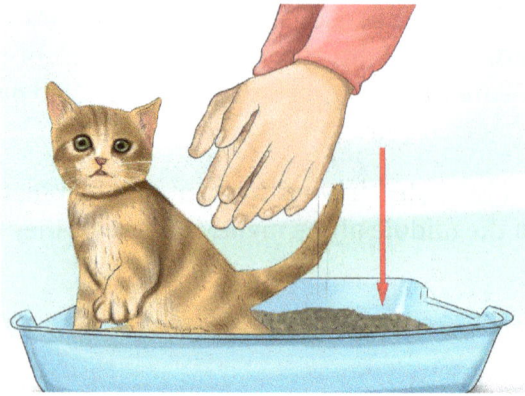

2. Place your cat in his litter box shortly after meals. You may also want to place your cat in his box shortly after he wakes up and after playing, as all of these are times most cats will want to excrete wastes. Putting your cat into the litter box during times he will likely need to relieve himself, such as after eating a meal or when he's just woken up, may help remind him to use the litter box every time he needs to go.

3. Keep a clean litter box. Cats will not want to use a litter box if it is dirty, and may resort to urinating or defecating around the house.

- Wear rubber gloves while handling cat feces to reduce the risk of contracting toxoplasmosis.

- Scoop out solid waste and clumps of urine-soaked litter everyday. Wash your hands thoroughly after handling soiled cat litter, even if you wore gloves.

- Do a thorough cleaning once a week. This entails dumping out old litter, washing the litter box with a mild detergent, thoroughly rinsing the soap away, drying the box completely, and pouring in a fresh layer of litter. You should only add about two to three inches (five to seven centimeters) of litter when refilling the box.

4. Use a litter your cat will enjoy. There are many different types of cat litter, made from a variety of different materials. The most important factor is finding a litter that your cat will want to use. Most cats prefer clumping, unscented litter. However, your cat may prefer something different, especially if he was adopted and grew accustomed to something in his former home. See what your cat responds to and adjust accordingly.

- The most common types of cat litter are clay litter, clumping litter, crystal/silica gel litter, and bio-degradable litter.

- Switch litters gradually, rather than abruptly, to minimize the shock and confusion to your cat. Mix a small amount of the new litter in with your cat's existing litter every day over the course of three to five days. If you change litters gradually, your cat shouldn't notice a difference.

- If your cat continuously relieves himself in a potted plant, he may prefer using soil instead of litter. This can be especially problematic in cats that used to live outdoors. Try lining your cat's litter box with potting soil, and see if he uses it.

5. Reward your cat for using the litter box. Give him praise immediately after he has finished using

the litter box. This will build positive habits and teach him that that is where he should be relieving himself.

6. Do not punish your cat for accidents outside the litter box. Negative reinforcement will not work, and may actually create a litter box avoidance problem in your cat.

- If your cat eliminates his waste outside the litter box, it's important to immediately wash that surface with an odor-neutralizing enzymatic cleaner. If your cat can smell his urine on the carpet, he might begin to associate that spot or that texture with going to the bathroom.

- If your cat passes solid waste outside the litter box, pick it up (with a paper towel or gloves) and place it in the litter box. This will give your cat scent-based cues to use the litter box next time.

- Try making unwanted elimination areas less desirable to your cat. If he has a part of the house that he tends to relieve himself in instead of using his litter box, leave tin foil or double-sided tape on the floor in that spot to discourage him from going there.

7. Try confinement training as a last resort. If your cat has a strong aversion to using his litter box and nothing else has worked, temporarily confining him in a single room with the litter box could instill an understanding in him to use the litter box.

- This should only be used as a last resort, when nothing else has worked.

- Do not confine your cat to a small room for extended periods of time. It is cruel to lock your cat up over long periods of time.

- Make sure your cat has food, water, and his bed in the room with the litter box. Keep the litter box on the opposite side of the room as the food, water, and bed.

- f he poops on the floor, scoop it up and put it in the tray to give him a scent mark to return to. If you cat is absolutely sold on a substrate, such as soil or carpet, and refuses to use the tray, then put that substrate in the tray. If necessary, purchase multiple pieces of carpet off cut and put it in the tray. Once the cat uses the tray with carpet in it, start to sprinkle cat litter over the carpet in the tray, to give the cat the idea. Replace sodden carpet with fresh in the tray.

Method 2

Training a Cat to Stop Biting

1. Play dead. If your cat gets too aggressive while playing and uses his teeth or nails, respond by immediately disengaging from the play activity, standing or sitting still, and ignoring him. Your cat will want to play, and when you deprive him of movement and interaction, he will quickly learn that he does not want that outcome.

- Never hit your cat. Likewise, do not yell at him or squirt him with water if he has bitten you. Over time, these negative responses can cause your cat to become fearful of you.

- Try changing the nature of your play if your cat becomes too aggressive. It's possible that he has slipped into hunting mode. Use a toy with a long string or handle to allow your cat to exercise his need to hunt without causing you injury or creating poor behavior.

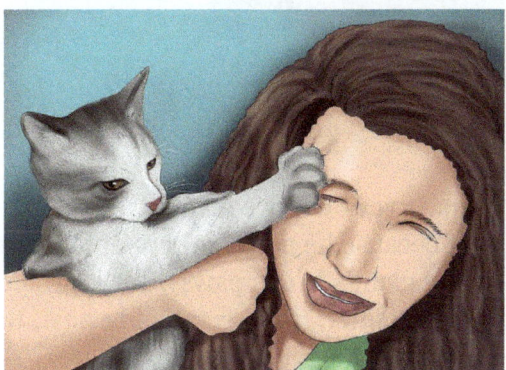

2. Respect your cat's boundaries. It's possible he bit or scratched you because you handled him

roughly or chased him into a defensive position. If your cat needs room, give him room. If he does not want to be handled, do not try to handle him.

3. Give your cat a hunting outlet. Your cat may not be getting enough exercise or enough outlets for his predatory instincts. Try giving him toys that he can flick, like a ball or a stuffed mouse. This will make him feel like he is hunting and catching. Better yet, use a toy with a string or pole, like a "fishing" toy, so that you and your cat can play together.

- Try using catnip. Many stuffed cat toys come with a velcro pouch to insert catnip, or you can simply sprinkle some catnip on the floor and let your cat roll around in it. About half of all cats won't find catnip desirable, but those that do will enjoy a short, safe burst of play time, followed by a period of ecstatic inactivity.

Method 3

Training a Cat to Stop Scratching Furniture

1. Give your cat a scratching post. If your cat is constantly scratching you or pieces of furniture, there's a chance that he's doing it because he needs to scratch. A cat scratches household items to mark his scent on that item (using glands in his paws), and to remove the sheath that naturally grows over his claws. Giving him an outlet, like a scratching post, to satisfy his scratching needs should alleviate some of this problem behavior.

- If you catch your cat scratching furniture, a carpet, or any other place he's not supposed to scratch, interrupt him with a sharp noise. Try clapping your hands or shaking a jar full of coins to startle your cat out of his scratching.

- Immediately direct your cat to his scratching post. By interrupting his scratching of furniture and moving him to an acceptable object like a scratching post, you are reinforcing for your cat the notion that some objects are okay to scratch, but not others.

2. Use citrus or menthol. Cats tend to dislike the smells of citrus and menthol. Rubbing a little bit of oil on the furniture your cat scratches the most could help prevent him from scratching there in the future.

- Soak several cotton balls in either citrus oil or a menthol-based muscle rub.

- Try dabbing the cotton ball on the legs and armrests of furniture your cat tends to target. Note that this will leave your furniture with a slight odor and may cause staining. Citrus oil may be less likely to stain. If you're concerned about the oils soaking through to your furniture, you may want to try simply taping the cotton balls onto the legs of couches and tables your cat tends to scratch.

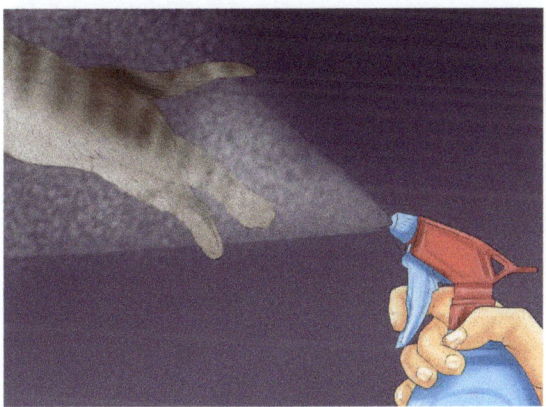

3. Use the squirt method. If your cat continues to pounce on your hands or feet, or destroy furniture around the house, it might be time to employ the water squirt method. Fill a spray bottle with clean, cold water. When the cat pounces, give him or her a quick squirt. Cats don't appreciate being sprayed with water, and they'll soon learn to associate this uncomfortable sensation with biting or scratching you.

- Be advised, however, that your cat will come to associate you with the unpleasant sensation of being sprayed with water. He may even come to fear you.

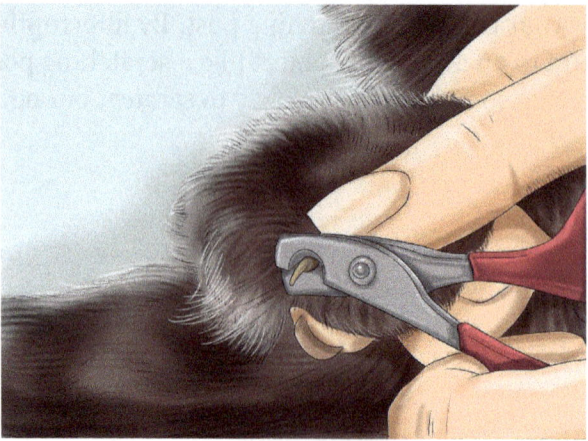

4. Do not get your cat declawed. No matter how bad of a scratching problem he has, getting your cat declawed will only cause worse problems. The process is incredibly painful for cats and can cause lasting problems like tissue necrosis, permanent pain, aversion to using the litter box, and increased aggression towards humans. Consult your vet on other ways to curb your cat's scratching if this behavior becomes problematic.

How to Teach a Cat to Do Tricks

Like many pets, cats can be trained to do tricks. Because they tend to be independent, teaching cats can take persistence, however. With positive reinforcement and patience, your cat can have a great time playing games and performing a variety of tricks.

Part 1

Learning How to Train your Cat

1. Get a supply of treats. Cats need to be constantly rewarded with tasty treats in order to learn

tricks. Keep plenty of your cat's favorite bite-sized treats on hand when trying to train it. Give your cat frequent treats when training it in short sessions. You can also vary treats frequently to keep your cat interested. Some good choices are:

- Diced chicken

- Bits of tuna

- Commercial cat treats

- Small pieces of dry food

2. Get your cat's attention. Your cat won't want to learn tricks if it's not in the mood. Starting by giving your cat a treat might get its attention. If your cat doesn't act interested in learning a particular trick, don't force it to play—just be patient and try again later.

3. Use a clicker. A pet clicker is a small device that makes a clicking sound. Each time your cat does something you want it to (like a trick), make the clicking sound and give it a treat. The sound and positive reinforcement (reward) of the treat condition your cat to repeat the behavior.

- Pet clickers can be found at pet supply stores. If you can't find one, you can try a pen that makes a clicking noise.

4. Keep training sessions short and frequent. Cats learn through repetition, so frequent training sessions will help them master a trick. Try repeating tricks several times each day. Keeping training sessions brief will also hold your cat's attention so it will want to keep trying.

5. Repeat tricks when training your cat. When your cat completes a trick, give it a treat. Then try to get your cat to repeat the trick 5-10 times in a row (giving it a treat each time), as long as it is interested. This repetition will encourage the behavior.

6. Don't use cue words until after the cat has learned a trick. For instance, if you want your cat to sit, don't use the word "sit" until it is used to doing the trick. This will help the cat associate the word specifically with the trick.

7. Teach one trick at a time. Positive reinforcement like praise and treats as your cat learns a trick will help it to master the behavior. Trying to teach it more than one trick at a time can confuse it, however, because it may not understand what behavior is being rewarded. Wait until your cat has mastered one trick before moving on to the next.

8. Do not punish your cat for not learning a trick. Cats learn when given rewards and positive reinforcement, not when they are punished. Scolding or punishing your cat when it doesn't complete a trick will only make it stressed or disinterested. If you cat doesn't act interested in learning a trick, or doesn't perform successfully, just try again later.

Part 2

Teach your Cat Specific Tricks

1. Teach your cat to sit. When your cat is on all four feet, hold a treat in front of its face to get its

attention. Slowly move it from in front of the cat's face to just between its ears. Many cats will follow the treat in the air and lower their rear end to get it. When your cat sits, positively reinforce its behavior by praising it and giving it the treat.

- If you cat's rear end doesn't quite touch the ground the first time, give it the treat anyway. Keep repeating this training and your cat can get better each time.

2. Teach your cat to "hi-five." First, encourage your cat to move its paw by giving it a treat each time it lifts the paw off of the ground. Then, put a treat in your hand (wrapped in your fist, for instance), and wait for your cat to use its paw to try and grab it out of your hand. Give the cat a treat as a reward when it does. Repeat this many times, gradually lifting your hand up higher each time until the behavior resembles giving a hi-five.

3. Train your cat to come when called. Try this training your cat for this trick at is mealtimes, because it will already be hungry. Call your cat's name and tap on its food bowl to get its attention. When your cat comes, praise them and give them a treat.

- When your cat gets used to coming when called, you can also use the command "come" for this trick.

- You can vary this trick by trying to train your cat to come from distances increasingly farther away, from outside to inside, etc.

4. Train your cat to touch an object. You can have your cat learn to touch an object like a toy or a sturdy surface that will not fall over. This trick is learned best after your cat has learned to sit. Once your cat is sitting next to the object, hold a treat near it to attract the cat. When the cat touches the object, give it a treat.

- Once your cat becomes interested in this trick, you can also train it to touch the object with a specific type of its body. For instance, if you want to train it to touch an object with its paw, wait to give your cat a treat until it does.

5. Train your cat to sit up on two legs. Hold a treat above your cat, but not so close that it can touch it. When your cat sits up on its hind legs, and reaches for the treat with its front paws, use a command like "sit" and give it the treat.

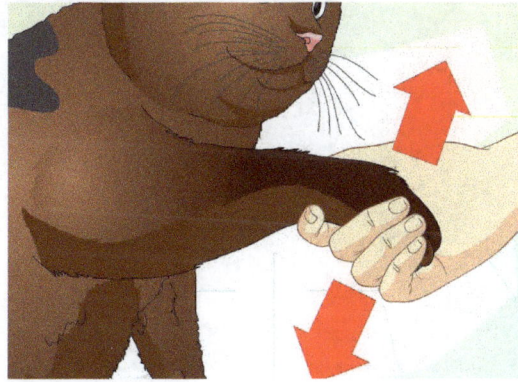

6. Teach your cat to shake hands. Sit in front of your cat and gently touch its paw. When it lifts

the paw off the ground, grasp it in yours as though you were shaking hands. Give your cat a treat immediately afterwards.

7. Train your cat to meow on command. Cats are capable of producing a wide range of vocal sounds (meows, chirps, trills, yowls, etc.), and they reserve most of them for communicating with humans. You can try training your cat to produce a meow or other sound on command. Just give your cat a treat when it makes the desired sound. After the cat begins to associate the treat with a reward, introduce a word like "meow" or "chirp" to create the command.

How to Train a Rabbit

Rabbits are very intelligent, social animals that can be trained quite easily. Unfortunately, many humans fail to train their rabbits, either because they use the wrong approach or they don't spend enough time on training. If you want to build a better relationship with your bunny, and train them right, you simply need to hop right in and get started!

Method 1

Understanding Rabbit Behavior

1. Understand what motivates your rabbit. Rabbits are very intelligent and eagerly respond to

incentives. This means that strong punishment, such as spanking or yelling at a rabbit, won't make it more cooperative. If you use incentives correctly, however, most rabbits will respond accordingly.

- Food is generally used as motivator, but toys may also be a reward for your rabbit.

- Rabbits are prey animals, so if they feel frightened they will usually flee and try to find somewhere to hide. If they exhibit this behavior, it means that you need to find a way to make them feel more comfortable and safe before attempting to train them.

2. Understand how a rabbit uses sight and smell. Bunnies do not see well directly in front of their faces. Their eyes are set far apart on the head and so they see to the side and far away better than up close.

- The rabbit will use scent and whisker feedback to detect anything in the immediate environment more so than sight, so you will want to place treats under the rabbit's nose and mouth.

- You may notice that rabbits change their head position as you get closer. This is an effort to see you better, like a person with bifocals trying to get the glasses and their eyes lined up to see.

- Rabbits are prey animals and need to see predators from far away, so that they can run and hide in time to save themselves. Because of this, before you touch it, you need to let the rabbit see and smell you. This will give you an easier time handling the rabbit. By letting it see and smell you, it can verify that you are not a predator, and therefore no danger to it.

3. Remember that kindness goes a long way with a rabbit. Rabbits respond to kindness and will make excellent companions who will respond positively to your voice and presence if you treat

them well. While you must have your rabbit's respect in order to train it, you'll be most successful if your rabbit also feels loved and comfortable in your presence.

- Not all rabbits enjoy being stroked, but some enjoy it so much that stroking can be an even better incentive than food. Spend plenty of quality time petting your rabbit, and attend to all its basic needs so that it feels secure and comfortable in your home.

- Never hold your bunny by the ears! Don't hurt your rabbit. Be kind and gentle to your fluffy friend and it will respond more positively to your training.

Method 2

Training your Rabbit to Follow Commands

1. Devote plenty of time to training. For best results plan on initially devoting a little time every day to training your rabbit. Two or three short sessions of 5 to 10 minutes at a time will keep your bunny interested in learning.

2. Use your rabbit's favorite treats. Since training is based on incentives, you'll need to find a treat that provides the most positive response. If you don't know what your rabbit's favorite treat is experiment a little. You can offer a new food, in small amounts to avoid digestive upset, once a day and watch the rabbit's response. If they leave it alone, then it won't work as a treat, but if the bunny munches it right down, you have a winner.

- If you're not sure if a particular food is safe for your rabbit, check with your veterinarian (one that is familiar with rabbits). Do not feed anything but vegetables, greens, or fruit to your bunny.

- If your rabbit is not used to eating much fruit or fresh greens, go easy on the amounts for a few weeks to avoid causing diarrhea or digestive upset.

- Your rabbit may like Blueberries or Kale or Carrot (try shreds of carrot) as a treat.

3. Get your rabbit in position for training. Stage your training in the area and situation where and when you will want the behavior to occur. For example, if you want to teach your rabbit to jump up on your lap when called, first put it near the couch. If you want to train it to go in its crate at night, train it around the appropriate time, and make sure its crate is positioned where it will normally be.

4. Have a plan. Start simple. Carefully plan what you want your rabbit to perform and break that task down into small steps. You will reward the rabbit after completing each new step. Once the rabbit is performing the task with regularity and confidence, give the command a name.

5. Give your rabbit a treat immediately when your rabbit does something you want to reward. If the rabbit sits up as you lift your hand above its head as if sitting up to beg, give the treat right away to reinforce "sit up." The reward will need to be given within 2-3 seconds of the behavior.

- If the rabbit does something else before you give the treat, you are reinforcing the wrong behavior.

- If you want to teach your rabbit to come when called, start its training by having it positioned very close to you. When it comes to you, give it the reward. Be consistent so that your fluffy companion knows why it's getting treats.

- Use the exact same commands, such as "Sit, (Your Rabbit's Name)," or "Up, (Your Rabbit's Name)," every time, so your rabbit will learn to recognize your requests and associate those exact words with getting a treat.

- Add praise to the act of giving the treat. For instance, "Good Sit" or "Good Up."

6. Keep providing the treats until your rabbit responds correctly nearly every time. When you're trying to teach a new skill, don't skimp on the rewards. You need to make sure you are thoroughly conditioning your rabbit.

- If you are training your rabbit to allow a harness to be placed, start with rewarding the bunny for going over to the harness on the floor and sniffing or touching the item. Work up to placing the harness on the bunny's back and rewarding them for staying still. Reward the bunny for calmly allowing you to lift up a front leg then work up to placing their foot through the appropriate part of the harness. Reward as you go and move slowly. Don't frighten or rush the rabbit. Once you have the harness in place, allow the rabbit to wear it for a few minutes at a time and take it off. Work up to having the rabbit drag the leash around the house before picking up the leash yourself.

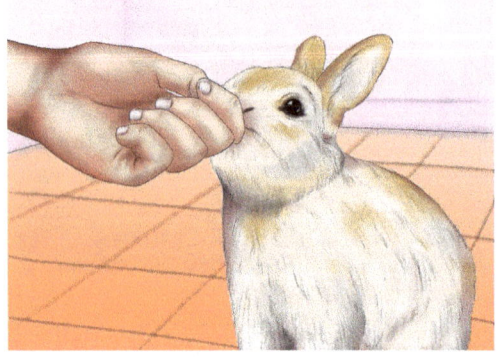

7. Consider using clicker training. Many people suggest using clickers to reinforce association.

Each time you feed the rabbit, click the clicker so that the rabbit associates the click with food. Then, when you're training, a click from the device tells the rabbit a treat is coming.

- Try to click right as the desired behavior is happening so the animal knows what it did to get the reward. Give the rabbit a treat or something else they enjoy within a few seconds of the click for each and every time you click, even if you click accidentally. The rabbit will learn that a click means a treat and try to earn clicks.

8. Wean your rabbit off the treats gradually. Once your rabbit has a skill down begin to give the treats less frequently. Give its reward once and then don't the next time, or give it a treat only every few times. Eventually you may not need treats at all.

- In time, reward your rabbit with petting and toys and only use food occasionally to keep the behavior strong.

- Rabbits like gentle strokes on their heads. Do not stroke the rabbit on its body; this is alarming to a rabbit. Be patient and take things slowly to avoid creating fear in your rabbit.

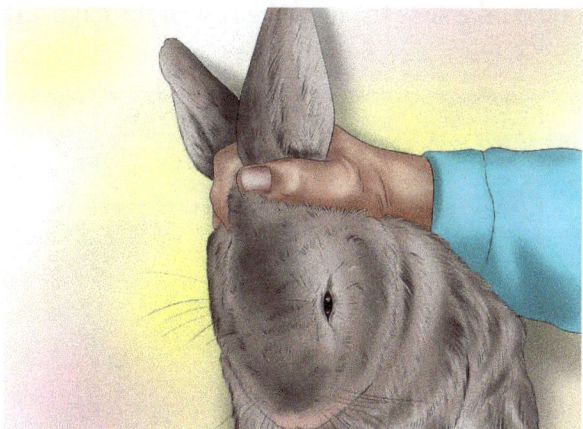

9. Reinforce the training as necessary. From time to time your rabbit may need to relearn a skill. That is, you may need to bring the incentives back. Don't be afraid to do so.

- Never scold, punish, shout or even say "no" to the rabbit during training. This is counter-productive and will make your rabbit more fearful and delay training.

Method 3

Training your Rabbit to use a Litter Box

1. Figure out where your rabbit is eliminating. They naturally choose a particular spot in the cage to eliminate. Because they use the same spot repeatedly, you can use this to your advantage.

2. Place a little of the dirty bedding in the litter box you bought for their cage. This will encourage the rabbit to use the litter box. Make sure to clean the rest of the cage after moving a bit of the dirty bedding.

3. Place the litter box in the place the rabbit has chosen to eliminate. There are litter boxes for rabbits made to fit in the corners of cages or you can use a rectangular version if the cage is large enough. If you position is right, the rabbit should naturally continue to use the same spot, only this time it will be in the litter box.

- Of course, larger litter boxes are possible when the rabbit is enjoying "bunny hop" time outside the cage.

Method 4

Addressing Rabbit Aggression

1. Make sure your rabbit knows who is in charge. Chances are your rabbit will want to rule the house. While you can't expect the kind of submission you can get from a dog, you must have the respect of your rabbit in order to train it.

- The most common way rabbits try to assert dominance is inappropriate nipping or biting you to try to herd you or get you to leave your sitting place. If this occurs, let out a short, loud, high-pitched squeal and either put your rabbit down on the floor (if it has jumped up where you're sitting) or pick it up and move it out of the way from you (if it is on the floor already). Do this firmly, but gently. You don't want to hurt your rabbit or make it fear you, you simply want to assert that you are in charge. If your rabbit continues the behavior, put it in its crate for a "time-out."

2. Address any aggression in your rabbit. First, approach your rabbit calmly so you do not elicit a fear response from the rabbit. Hang out on the floor with your rabbit. Have some treats on the floor. Reward the rabbit for coming closer to you. Leave your hand down. If the rabbit comes up to you and does not seem afraid or does not try to bite you, try to gently stroke the rabbit's head for just a few seconds.

- If you do not back down and avoid the reflex to "run away" if the bunny charges you, the rabbit will learn that this behavior does not work to intimidate you.

- Never hit the rabbit. You and your hands are the sources of food and pleasure, like petting on top of the rabbit's head.

- If you are afraid of being injured, wear long pants, shoes, long sleeves and gloves if necessary to protect yourself from bites.

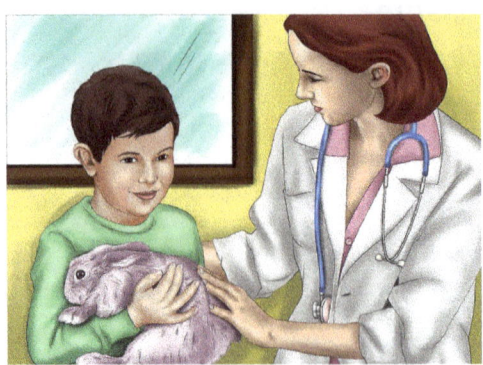

3. Investigate whether your rabbit's aggression has an underlying cause. A change in your rabbit's behavior, including aggression, should be investigated to eliminate the chance that there is a medical issue causing the problem. Consult with a veterinarian familiar with rabbits to rule out pain, for instance, as a cause for misbehavior.

- Hormones can also influence bunny behavior and having your rabbit spayed or neutered may help decrease territorial aggression, for instance.

How to Train your Bird

Birds are very clever animals, and can make very fun and interesting pets. With patience and practice, you can train your bird to do different tricks, and even train him where to go to the bathroom! Training your bird is an excellent way to bond with him, so have fun and enjoy the process.

Method 1

Training your Bird to Step up and Down

1. Acclimate your bird to your hand. Training your bird to step up has many benefits, including

decreasing his fear towards you, establishing your authority, and decreasing his territorial behavior. Your bird may not be immediately comfortable with stepping up on your hand, so he will need to first get used to your hand. Begin by placing your hand near the outside of his cage for about a week, and talking to him in a gentle voice.

- Once your bird is comfortable with the sight of your hand, place your hand in his cage in a slow and non-threatening manner. It may take another week before he is comfortable with your hand inside his cage.

2. Place a treat in your hand. Your bird may be comfortable with your hand inside his cage, but he still may not want to step on it. Entice him to come closer with a treat. Reward him with the treat when he steps closer, even if he does not actually touch your hand at first.

- It may take several tries before your bird is ready to take the treat from your hand. Be patient with him.

- Spray millet is a great bird treat.

3. Hold your index finger like a perch. Once your bird is at ease with your hand being inside his cage, position your index finger like a perch (finger pointed out). Slowly move your hand closer to your bird. Next, gently press your finger against your bird's lower chest to encourage him to step up onto your finger.

- Use a verbal cue ('step up' or 'up') as you press your finger against his chest.

- Reward your bird immediately with verbal praise ('good bird') and a treat when he steps up onto your finger.

- Your bird may not initially understand that he is supposed to step up onto your hand. If he runs away from your hand, entice him to your finger with some spray millet rather than following him around his cage with your hand.

4. Take your bird from his cage. Slowly take him out of his cage when he is perched on your finger. Be careful to avoid any toys or perches as you move your hand outside of his cage.

- Do not be surprised if your bird suddenly panics and flies off your finger. If he does so, calmly walk to him and encourage him to step up again. Repeat this each time he flies off your finger.

- If your bird seems distressed or exhausted, stop your training session and return him to his cage.

- Hold your bird at your chest level when you have him outside of his cage. This will establish your authority over him.

5. Use your hands like a ladder. To add a challenge to this trick, encourage your bird to step up

multiple times. Position your free hand above the hand on which he is perched. With the index finger of your free hand positioned like a perch, gently press against his chest and say your verbal cue.

- Repeat this several times, rewarding your bird each time that he steps up.

- You can also gently lift and stroke his toes to increase his comfort level of being perched on your finger.

6. Command your bird to step down. Slowly move your bird back into his cage with him still perched on your finger. Position him such that he will be facing forward in his cage. If you will be placing him on a perch, make sure that your finger is below the perch.

- Use a verbal cue ('step down' or 'down') as he steps down, even though he will be stepping up onto his perch.

- Reward your bird when he steps off your finger.

Method 2

Training your Bird with a Towel

1. Use a white or light-colored towel. Towel training your bird is useful if you need to groom him,

administer medication, or handle him when he is injured. Bright-colored towels may be alarming to your bird, so lighter-colored towels are preferable.

- Place the towel on the bottom of his cage.

- It may be helpful to first leave the towel in your bird's cage for several days to allow him to get used to its presence.

2. Encourage your bird to step onto the towel. Similar to your hand, your bird may not be immediately comfortable with the towel. Place a treat on the towel to entice your bird to step on it.

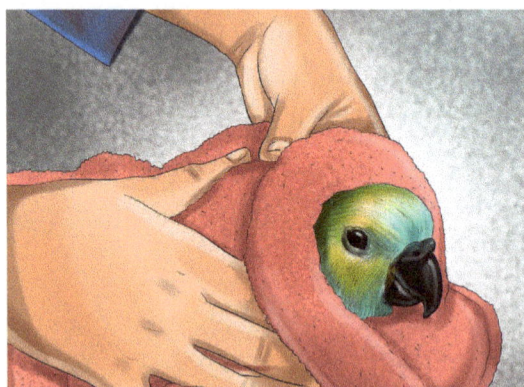

3. Wrap your bird in the towel. When your bird is standing on the towel, gently wrap him up in it from behind. It is very important that you wrap him up in such a way that he cannot bite you, but is still able to breathe comfortably. To begin, gently place your thumb and middle finger of the hand holding the towel on each side of his neck.

- Do not put any pressure on your bird's neck with the thumb and middle finger.

- Place the index finger of the hand holding the towel on top his head to keep him still.

- Wrap your bird's wings inside the towel to prevent him from struggling and flapping his wings.

- Make sure that the towel is not rubbing your bird's eyes.

- Do not put any pressure on his chest. Pressure on his chest could cause him to suffocate.

- Try to rest your bird in the palm of the hand holding the towel. You may need to use both hands if you have a larger bird.

4. Unwrap your bird. Ensure that your bird's feet are touching the bottom of his cage. With him stabilized on a solid surface, gently release your fingers from the sides of his neck and release him from the towel. He will probably ruffle his feathers and might even vocalize when you release him.

- Allow your bird to relax and get comfortable again.

- Reward him with a treat if he was still and did not try to bite you when you held him in a towel.

Method 3

House Training your Bird

1. Choose a command. You may not have realized it, but you can house train a bird! Other than the benefit of cleaning up fewer messes, house training your bird will enhance your bond with him and allow you to have a better understanding of his body language. The command you choose should be short, such as 'go potty' or 'go poop.'

- Each person in your household should use the same command.

2. Select where you want your bird to defecate. Your bird's cage probably seems like an obvious place for your bird to defecate. However, if you have him outside of his cage often, you may want to choose another object, such as newspaper or a wastebasket, where he can relieve himself.

- Whichever location/object you choose, use it consistently as you are house training your bird.

3. Observe your bird's body language. Your bird will let you know when he has to go to the bathroom. For example, he may crouch his body. He may also move his tail, fluff his feathers, or step backward.

- Being able to recognize this body language will let you be one step ahead of him and give him the command before he defecates.

- It would also be helpful to make a note of when he usually goes to the bathroom. Most birds will defecate first thing in the morning, after meals, and when they are taken out of and placed back into their cages.

- Smaller birds tend to go the bathroom more frequently than larger birds.

4. Move your bird to the 'bathroom' location. As soon as you see your bird making motions to relieve himself, command him to step up on your finger and move him to the area where he should defecate. Give him the verbal command and reward him immediately after he relieves himself.

- Practice this each time your bird needs to defecate so that he forms the association between defecating in the right location and being rewarded for it.

- Do not punish him if he defecates in the wrong location. Doing this may backfire—he might defecate in the wrong place just to get your attention.

Method 4

Teaching your Bird to Talk

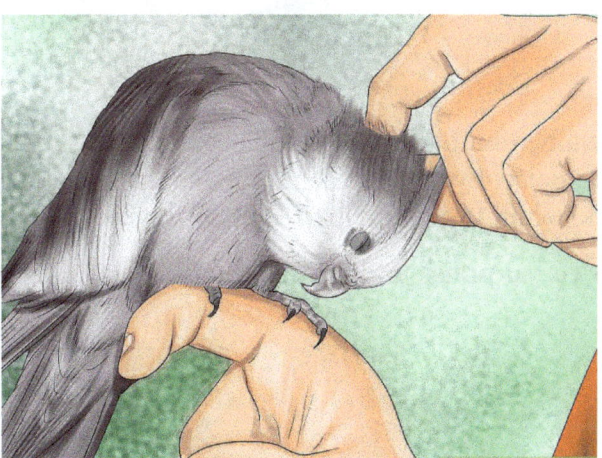

1. Show your bird you love him. Teaching your bird to talk enhances your ability to communicate with him and vice versa. Before encouraging him to speak, though, it is important to communicate your love to him. Scratching your bird behind his neck while saying 'I love you' will let him know you love him.

- You can also kiss his beak and say the word 'kiss.'

- You can add his name to the 'I love you' statement so that your bird learns his name.

2. Say a word with its corresponding action. It will be easier for your bird to learn words if he is able to link the words with a specific action. For example, say 'scratch' when you scratch your bird's neck. You can also say 'good morning' and 'good night' as you respectively greet him in the morning and go to bed at night.

- When you feed him, say the name of the food as you are giving it to him.

- In time, you may notice your bird responding to your words with his body language (e.g., lifting his wing when you say 'scratch').

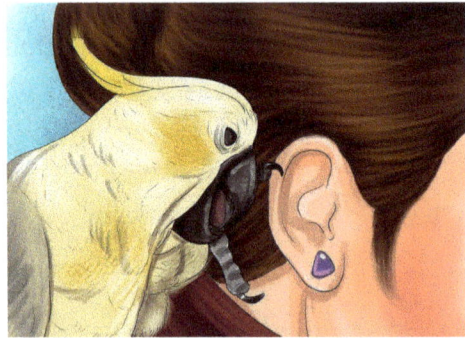

3. Listen to your bird. Initially, your bird's words will probably not sound very clear. He may make a mumbling or whispering noise. Even if you cannot make out the words, eagerly encourage him and repeat the words back to him to get him excited about saying them.

- Reward him with verbal praise and a treat when he attempts to say the words you are teaching him.

4. Monitor how you speak around your bird. Birds are more likely to learn words that are spoken

enthusiastically. If there is a word or phrase that you don't want your bird to repeat, do not say it in an enthusiastic voice around him—he will probably pick up on it and repeat it when it is socially inappropriate for him to do so.

- The words you want your bird to learn should be the only ones spoken in an enthusiastic voice when you are around him.

5. Respond to your bird as he speaks to you. Your bird may forget the words or phrases you teach him if you do not react to him when he says them. He may also forget them if you do not continue to say them to him.

- Your positive reaction to him will encourage him to continue talking to you.

- If there is a word or phrase that you do not want your bird to say anymore, do not react to him when he says it.

Method 5

Learning General Bird-Training Tips

1. Get your bird to be comfortable with you. This can be particularly important for older or re-homed birds who have previously been mistreated or improperly trained. Doing quiet activities around your bird, such as reading or watching TV, will allow him to get comfortable with your presence without having to interact with you.

- It may take your bird several weeks before he is comfortable with you. If that is the case, be patient with him and move at his pace.

- Quietly talking to him can also help your bird feel more at ease with you.

2. Pick a good location to train your bird. The area where you train your bird should be quiet and free of distractions. In the training area, make sure to close all windows and doors and turn off any fans.

- Your bird's cage could be one of your bird's distractions.

- Ideally, the cage should be out of sight. However, a bird who is insecure or easily frightened may benefit from having his cage where he can see it.

3. Keep the training sessions short. As with other pets, long training sessions can lead to exhaustion or even boredom in birds. Training sessions with your bird should last for 10 minutes, two to three times a day.

- Your bird may also become aggressive during his training sessions. He may show his aggression by vocalizing, flapping his wings, or biting you. End the training session if he is displaying aggressive behavior.

- You should always end the training session on a good note, such as giving your bird verbal praise or a treat.

4. Acclimate your bird to your training props. Depending on which command you are teaching him, you may need props during the training session. Allowing your bird to become comfortable with the props first should make the training sessions go more smoothly. Placing the props in his cage for a few days will help your bird acclimate to them.

- Playing with the props yourself may pique your bird's interest in them.

5. Give your bird treats. Positive reinforcement is very helpful when training a bird. Treats are a great way to reinforce your bird's positive behavior. To keep from being bitten, hold your fingers to the side of the treat when you give it to him.

- Your bird may mistake your fingers as a nut and bite them on accident.

- Examples of healthy snacks for birds are strawberries, mangoes, and peppers.

- Spray millet is another great treat for birds.

- Whichever treat you use, reserve it only for training purposes.

6. Be consistent when using commands. Using the same command each time you are teaching your bird a new trick will help him learn the trick more easily. If there are multiple members of your household, it is important for each person to use the same command for the same trick.

7. Be patient. Your bird may take a long time to learn certain tricks. If this is the case, be patient with him as he learns. Be mindful, though, that your bird may take a long time to learn a trick because he does not want to learn it at all.

- If your bird is getting frustrated or starts acting aggressively, it may be time to consider teaching him another trick.

8. Do not punish your bird. Punishment is not effective for birds. In fact, the punishment may

seem like attention to your bird, and he will continue to demonstrate the bad behavior. Positive reinforcement, such as verbal praise or treats, is much more effective at training your bird than punishment.

9. Discourage biting and screaming behavior. Biting and screaming are two undesirable behaviors that your bird may demonstrate. If your bird bites you, gently blow a puff of air in his face and firmly say 'no.' Do not give your bird a timeout if he bites you—he may learn that biting you is a way to get you to leave him alone.

- If your bird starts to scream, stand close by and talk to him in quiet and soothing voice until he calms down.

- Do not give your bird treats if he bites you or screams.

10. Discourage biting and chewing on furniture. Bitter apple spray is an effective way of deterring your bird from inappropriate biting or chewing. Spray it wherever you notice these undesirable behaviors. He will eventually learn the places where he should not bite or chew.

- Bitter apple spray is available at your local pet store.

How to Travel with your Pets

Travel with your pets can be either be an enjoyable or nerve-wracking experience for both you and your pet. Your preparation will determine which it is.

Steps

1. Decide when and where you will be traveling and how long you will be gone.

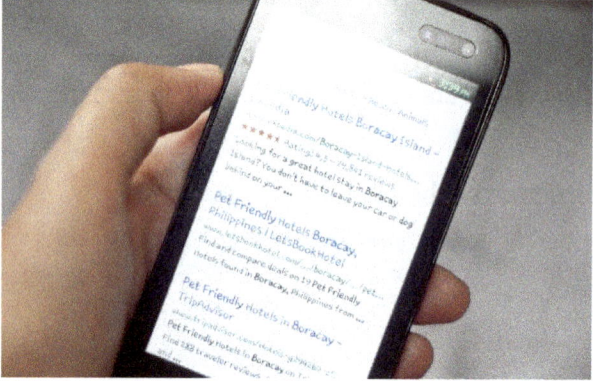

2. Research if taking your pet is safe and reasonable

3. Check with where you will be staying to see if pets are welcome. This can include calling the

hotel or family member. Just because you've had pets there before doesn't mean the policy hasn't changed. Be a polite pet owner and ask.

- Make sure your pet is well-groomed before you stay somewhere else.

- Bring doggie bags to clean up after your dog.

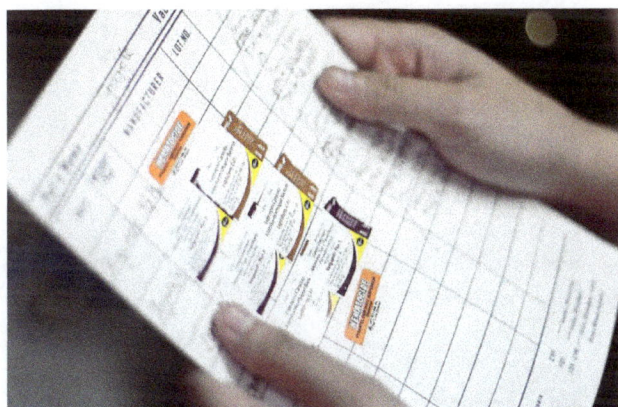

4. Make sure your pet is up to date on all vaccinations and you have a copy of the shot record. Schedule vet appointment if necessary.

5. Determine the best mode of travel for you and your pets. The following steps will guide you through traveling safely with your pets.

Taking Care of Pets

Giving care to pets is a primary task of pet daycare centers. Being updated about each pet's needs and requirements, such as diet and exercise is very important. Providing first aid, if necessary, is also crucial. The topics discussed in the chapter are of great importance to broaden the existing knowledge on pet care.

Pet

A cat and dog, two popular pet species.

A pet or companion animal is an animal kept primarily for a person's company, protection, or entertainment rather than as a working animal, sport animal, livestock, or laboratory animal. Popular pets are often noted for their attractive appearances, and their loyal or playful personalities.

Pets provide their owners (or guardians) physical and emotional benefits. Walking a dog can supply both the human and pet with exercise, fresh air, and social interaction. Pets can give companionship to elderly adults who do not have adequate social interaction with other people, as well as to other people who are living alone. There is a medically approved class of therapy animals, mostly dogs or cats, that are brought to visit confined humans, such as children in hospitals or elders in nursing homes. Pet therapy utilizes trained animals and handlers to achieve specific physical, social, cognitive, and emotional goals with patients.

The most popular pets are likely dogs and cats but people also keep house rabbits, ferrets; rodents such as gerbils, hamsters, chinchillas, fancy rats, and guinea pigs; avian pets, such as canaries, parakeets, corvids, parrots, and chickens; reptile pets, such as turtles, lizards and snakes;

aquatic pets, such as goldfish, tropical fish and frogs; and arthropod pets, such as tarantulas and hermit crabs.

Some scholars, ethicists and animal rights organizations have raised concern over pet-keeping with regards to the autonomy and objectification of nonhuman animals.

Legalities

States, cities, and towns in Western nations commonly enact local ordinances to limit the number or kind of pets a person may keep personally or for business purposes. Prohibited pets may be specific to certain breeds (such as pit bulls or Rottweilers), they may apply to general categories of animals (such as livestock, exotic animals, wild animals, and canid or felid hybrids), or they may simply be based on the animal's size. Additional or different maintenance rules and regulations may also apply. Condominium associations and owners of rental properties also commonly limit or forbid tenants' keeping of pets.

The keeping of animals as pets can cause concerns with regard to animal rights and welfare. Pets have commonly been considered private property, owned by individual persons. However, many legal protections have existed (historically and today) with the intention of safeguarding pets' (and other animals') well-being. Since the year 2000, a small but increasing number of jurisdictions in North America have enacted laws redefining pet's *owners* as *guardians*. Intentions have been characterized as simply changing attitudes and perceptions (but not legal consequences) to working toward legal personhood for pets themselves. Some veterinarians and breeders have opposed these moves. The question of pets' legal status can arise with concern to purchase or adoption, custody, divorce, estate and inheritance, injury, damage, and veterinary malpractice.

Pet Popularity

A Maine Coon kitten aged ten weeks

There are approximately 86.4 million pet cats in the United States, approximately 78.2 million pet dogs in the United States, and 5.3 million house rabbits. The two most popular pets in most Western countries have been cats and dogs. In the United States, a 2007–2008 survey showed that dog-owning households outnumbered those owning cats, but that the total number of pet cats was higher than that of dogs. The same was true for 2011. In 2013, pets outnumbered children four to one in the United States.

Guinea pigs

Pet Labrador, being petted

A Maltese puppy

Most popular pets in the U.S (millions)				
Pet	**Global population**	**U.S. population**	**U.S. inhabited households**	**U.S. average per inhabited household**
Cat	202	93.6	38.2	2.45
Dog	171	77.5	45.6	1.70
Fish	N/A	171.7	13.3	12.86
Small mammals	N/A	15.9	5.3	3.00
Birds	N/A	15.0	6.0	2.50
Reptiles & amphibians	N/A	13.6	4.7	2.89
Equine	N/A	13.3	3.9	3.41

Effects on Pets' Health

Keeping animals as pets may be detrimental to their health if certain requirements are not met. An important issue is inappropriate feeding, which may produce clinical effects. The consumption of chocolate or grapes by dogs, for example, may prove fatal.

Certain species of houseplants can also prove toxic if consumed by pets. Examples include philodendrons and Easter lilies (which can cause severe kidney damage to cats) and poinsettias, begonia, and aloe vera (which can sicken or, in extreme cases, kill dogs).

Housepets, particularly dogs and cats in industrialized societies, are also highly susceptible to obesity. Overweight pets have been shown to be at a higher risk of developing diabetes, liver problems, joint pain, kidney failure, and cancer. Lack of exercise and high-caloric diets are considered to be the primary contributors to pet obesity.

Effects of Pets on their Caregiver's Health

Health Benefits

Pets might have the ability to stimulate their caregivers, in particular the elderly, giving people someone to take care of, someone to exercise with, and someone to help them heal from a physically or psychologically troubled past. Animal company can also help people to preserve acceptable levels of happiness despite the presence of mood symptoms like anxiety or depression. Having a pet may also help people achieve health goals, such as lowered blood pressure, or mental goals, such as decreased stress. There is evidence that having a pet can help a person lead a longer, healthier life. In a 1986 study of 92 people hospitalized for coronary ailments, within a year 11 of the 29 patients without pets had died, compared to only 3 of the 52 patients who had pets. Having pet(s) was shown to significantly reduce triglycerides, and thus heart disease risk, in the elderly. A study by the National Institute of Health found that people who owned dogs were less likely to die as a result of a heart attack than those who didn't own one. There is some evidence that pets may have a therapeutic effect in dementia cases. Other studies have shown that for the elderly, good health may be a requirement for having a pet, and not a result. Dogs trained to be guide dogs can help people with vision impairment. Dogs trained in the field of Animal-Assisted Therapy (AAT) can also benefit people with other disabilities.

Pets in Long-term Care Institutions

People residing in a long-term care facility, such as a hospice or nursing home, experience health benefits from pets. Pets help them to cope with the emotional issues related to their illness. They also offer physical contact with another living creature, something that is often missing in an elder's life. Pets for nursing homes are chosen based on the size of the pet, the amount of care that the breed needs, and the population and size of the care institution. Appropriate pets go through a screening process and, if it is a dog, additional training programs to become a therapy dog. There are three types of therapy dogs: facility therapy dogs, animal-assisted therapy dogs, and therapeutic visitation dogs. The most common therapy dogs are therapeutic visitation dogs. These dogs are household pets whose handlers take time to visit hospitals, nursing homes, detention facilities, and rehabilitation facilities. Different pets require varying amounts of attention and care; for example, cats may have lower maintenance requirements than dogs.

Connection with Community

In addition to providing health benefits for their owners, pets also impact the social lives of their owners and their connection to their community. There is some evidence that pets can facilitate social interaction. Assistant Professor of Sociology at the University of Colorado at Boulder, Leslie Irvine has focused her attention on pets of the homeless population. Her studies of pet ownership among the homeless found that many modify their life activities for fear of losing their pets. Pet ownership prompts them to be and act responsibly, with many making a deliberate choice not to drink or use drugs, and to avoid contact with substance abusers or those involved in any criminal activity for fear of being separated from their pet. Additionally, many refuse housing in shelters if their pet is not allowed to stay with them.

Health Risks

Health risks that are associated with pets include:

- Aggravation of allergies and asthma caused by dander and fur or feathers

- Falling injuries. Tripping over pets, especially dogs, causes more than 86,000 falls serious enough to prompt a trip to the emergency room each year in the United States. Among elderly and disabled people, these falls have resulted in life-threatening injuries and broken bones.

- Injury, mauling, and sometimes death caused by pet bites and attacks
- Disease or parasites due to animal hygiene problems, lack of appropriate treatment, and undisciplined behavior (faeces and urine)
- Stress caused by behaviour of animals

Environmental Impact

Pets have a considerable environmental impact, especially in countries where they are common or held in high densities. For instance, the 163 million dogs and cats kept in the United States consume about 20% of the amount of dietary energy that humans do and an estimated 33% of the animal-derived energy. They produce about 30% ± 13%, by mass, as much feces as Americans, and through their diet, constitute about 25–30% of the environmental impacts from animal production in terms of the use of land, water, fossil fuel, phosphate, and biocides. Dog and cat animal product consumption is responsible for release of up to 64 ± 16 million tons CO_2-equivalent methane and nitrous oxide, two powerful greenhouse gasses. Americans are the largest pet owners in the world, but pet ownership in the US has considerable environmental costs.

Types

While many people have kept many different species of animals in captivity over the course of human history, only a relative few have been kept long enough to be considered domesticated. Other types of animals, notably monkeys, have never been domesticated but are still commonly sold and kept as pets. There are also inanimate objects that have been kept as "pets", either as a form of game, or humorously (e.g. the Pet Rock or Chia Pet).

Domesticated

Domesticated pets are the most common types of pet. A *domesticated animal* is any animal that has been tamed and made fit for a human environment. They have consistently been kept in captivity over a long enough period of time that they exhibit marked differences in behavior and appearance from their wild relatives.

Mammals

A pet rabbit

A pet hedgehog with albinism.

Wild Animals

Wild animals are often kept as pets. The term wild in this context specifically applies to any species of animal which has not undergone a fundamental change in behavior to facilitate a close co-existence with humans. Some species listed here may have been bred in captivity for a considerable length of time, but are still not recognized as domesticated.

The Hiran Minar near Lahore, Pakistan was built in the 17th century by the Mughal Emperor Jahangir as a funerary monument in honor of his pet deer.

The Pasha's Favourite Tiger, oil painting by Rudolph Ernst

Arthropods

- Ants
- Caterpillars
- Centipedes
- Crabs and hermit crabs
- Millipedes
- Praying mantises
- Stick insects
- Sea-Monkeys
- Triops
- Tarantulas and other spiders

How to Take Care of your Pet

Maybe you have a pet or are thinking of getting one. It's important that you understand how to take care of a pet properly. Many pets are very loving creatures, and they are relying on you for proper care. Caring for a pet isn't that hard, but it can be time consuming, so make sure you're prepared to do it before you get one.

Part 1

Preparing for your Pet

1. Research the type of pet, so you can make sure the pet fits into your environment and lifestyle. It is critical that you do adequate research before buying the pet. Different animals have different

needs regarding care (for example, tropical fish cannot be treated the same way as cold water fish), and even within the same species, different breeds can have different needs.

- If you are buying a dog, then buying a high energy, large breed such as a wolfhound would be unsuitable if you live in a small apartment or spend all day at work and have nowhere to let the dog roam in the day. Focus on the pet's needs, not your wants.

- If you want an animal like a snake instead, research is still important. It is critical that the snake has enough space to crawl around in and a heat source (such as a lightbulb).

- If you're leading an active life, choose a dog. If you are away from home a lot, though, choose a cat or some other free-roaming animal. If you just want an animal to look at and don't want to interact with it directly, or don't have lots of time, choose a fish or a snake, or other creepy-crawlies.

2. Choose your breed carefully, especially if you have children. It's a mistake to just decide "I want a dog" (or any other animal) and to buy the animal without considering the needs and requirements of the breed.

- Some breeds are natural shepherds, which makes them great for 1 person, but some breeds (Border Collie, for example) have the sheep-herding instinct in their blood. This means that when a child roams too far from the rest of the "herd," the collie will try to get it back. How does it do it with the sheep? It bites them. This may result in grave injuries to children. Please do your research on how breeds behave.

- It is important that a pet lives in an environment where it will be comfortable, safe and provided with what it needs. Some animals are very adaptable, such as cats, which can live happily in environments ranging from farm land to city centers, while others have more specific needs. For example, horses must have a lot of pastureland and somewhere safe to shelter.

- For animals that will roam the house, not being confined to tanks or cages, they will need places to sleep that are out of the way of general household traffic, where they can lie without being disturbed, such as the corner of a room. If they are a cat that will often be shut indoors, then it is also important that they have a litter tray that is regularly cleaned out.

3. Be realistic about your budget, and your ability to shoulder responsibilities. Some pets are more expensive than other pets, and you need to be honest with yourself about whether you can afford the pet - and whether you have the time and maturity to handle it.

- Costs associated with pets include set-up supplies. Depending on the kind of pet, you might need a crate, an aquarium, and leashes.

- Don't forget the ongoing costs of caring for a pet. You need to factor in the cost of regular food purchases, but also whether you can afford to take your pet to the veterinarian for pre-ventative care (like shots), not just emergency care. That's essential to keep the pet healthy, and it can be quite costly.

Part 2

Keeping your Pet Healthy

1. Exercise your pet if it's the kind of pet that needs it, such as a dog. Figure out the exercise needs (if any) of the pet before you buy it, and consider whether your lifestyle gives you enough time to meet them.

- Some pets don't require you to do much beyond providing them with a safe place to move about, such as buying a run for a rabbit, and making sure the tank is large enough for fish. But other pets must be exercised.

- Dogs require a more hands-on approach to exercise because they need to be walked regularly. Making sure your pet gets enough exercise can help prevent aggression and destructive behaviors.

2. Watch your pet's diet carefully. Many foods that are edible for humans can be inappropriate for animals, making them ill when they consume them, so it is important to research what foods your pet can not eat as well as those they can eat.

- Overfeeding is as harmful as underfeeding, so it is important that your pet gets the amount of food it needs and not too much extra. For some animals, dietary requirements may change with the season; for example, if you have horses or other grazing animals, they will often require more hay during the seasons when there is less grass.

- Look at pet food labels to make sure you are purchasing food for your pet that is properly nutritious. Research which food could harm your pet.

- It is vital that all pets have a constant water supply. Check water bowls at least once a day to ensure that they have enough water and that the water is clean and not contaminated.

3. Consider whether your pet needs to be groomed. Many animals will largely take care of themselves, only really needing to be groomed or bathed when they manage to get very messy. Others, such as long-haired dogs or cats, may need regular grooming.

- It is a good idea to desensitize your pet to being groomed or bathed from an early age. When brushing fur, ensure any brush used on the face is soft, and if brushing long, tangled fur, take the time to work out knots gently rather than tugging. You can buy brushes for pets at pet stores.

- When bathing your pet, make sure that the water is lukewarm and that the products you use do not cause an allergic reaction - buying specialist shampoos is not always necessary, but heavily perfumed products may cause a rash for many animals.

- Consider taking your pet to a professional groomer if you aren't sure you are competent to do it. You don't want to accidentally injure the pet.

4. Monitor your pet for illness and injury. As pets cannot tell us when they are ill or injured, it is up to us to keep an eye on them and look out for any signs of injury.

- Knowing your pet's normal behavior is very important; if they are sick or injured, they will often act unusually, such as sleeping more, going off their food, etc. If they begin to act oddly, check them for any injuries and keep an eye on their food and water intake; if they stop eating or drinking, or they have obvious wounds that are concerning you, then take them to the vet.

- Make sure that your pet has all of the proper vaccines and other preventative medication suggested by your veterinarian, such as heart worm pills for some dogs.

Part 3

Giving your Pet Attention

1. Train your pet if it's the kind of pet that needs it. A major part of caring for a pet is training. Training is essential for the safety of the animal and the people who interact with it.

- If you have an apartment cat, the litter box is very important from the start. You have to teach your cat to use the litter box and to think of it as its only place to do the necessary business. The litter box needs frequent cleaning (once or twice a day, depending on the cat). Feeding is approximately 2 or 3 times a day, again, depending on the cat. Water should be supplied continuously.

- Dogs need to be trained so they understand proper behavior, such as where to go to the bathroom and not to jump on people when they enter the house. It's important that the owner establishes control, but never in an abusive or harmful way to the animal.

2. Make time for your pet. Some animals require more attention than others, so the amount of time they need is often relative. Just be sure than you are capable of fulfilling whatever that need may be.

- Try to take a little time out of each day to spend with your pet, even if it's just sitting down with them. More often than not, your pet would be more than happy to relax with you.

- Dogs should be walked, and hamsters need time to run around in their balls. Play should be fun for both your pet and you, but make sure it is safe and monitored at all times.

- Research whether your pet breed needs to socialize with other animals. Play with it - dogs are very social animals so they need to spend time with their owners. With toys or simply chasing him around is enough for exercising. Dogs have a natural craving for chewing things, so buy a chewing toy to keep him entertained.

3. Love your pet. Love is what your relationship with your pet has to be about. Show him or her your affection by petting and playing.

- Your pet will be a member of your family, so treat it like one. A good cuddle will do the both of you good. Pets respond to the tone of people's voices as well as touch.

- Horses need attention. Like wild horses, if you don't love them properly, they pretty much turn into mustang. Give them a treat once in a while, take a walk with them, or ride them for fun.

- Train a pet with positive reinforcement, never cruelty or abuse.Keep your pet and its environment clean.

- If you have a small animal, clean their cage weekly. You're not showing your pet love if you let it sit in filth. If you have a dog, vacuum fur regularly from the house and wash their dog bed from time to time. Neglecting to clean your pet could result in infection, so keep on top of its cleanliness!

How to Take Care of a Cat

With their playful personalities, affectionate behavior, and adorable faces, cats can be the ideal pet. But, despite popular opinion, cats are *not* maintenance-free! To keep your cat healthy and happy, you need to know how to take care of him and provide the best possible life for your new friend.

Part 1

Getting a Cat

1. Decide if you want a kitten or a full-grown cat. Kittens are adorably tempting, but be honest with yourself about whether you'll be able to match that energy level. Shelters are full of loving adult cats who have a much harder time getting adopted. An adult cat will be calmer and quieter than a kitten, but may also have behavioral issues from its previous life. Adult cats may also have medical

conditions you'll have to address sooner than you would with a kitten. Also, kittens often scratch very painfully; Decide if you want that.

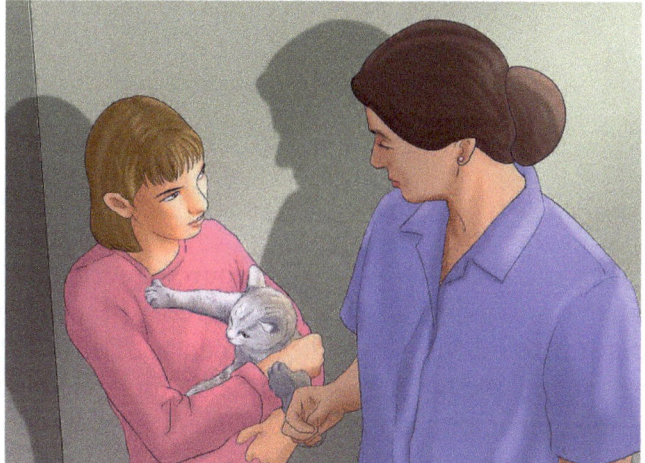

2. Consider medical concerns that may come with a specific cat. If you have your eye on one cat in particular, ask about its medical history to see if it requires any long-term care. Would you be able to afford this cat's medical needs?

- Even if the cat is healthy, consider its breed. Purebred cats from different breeds can have their own genetic problems to overcome. For example, flat-faced cats like Manx and Scottish folds often develop breathing problems.

- Purebred cats are more likely to have genetic medical problems than non-pedigreed cats.

3. Consider the amount of time you have for a cat. While a cat doesn't need daily walking like a dog, don't be fooled into thinking that cats aren't a time commitment. They're still active pets that need a lot of play, and affectionate companions who demand attention. You'll also spend time cleaning the litter box and giving the cat structured meals.

- The average lifespan of an indoor cat is 13-17 years, so be aware that you're making a long-term commitment to a new family member.

4. Calculate whether you can afford a cat. The one-time purchase fee for a cat can range from $45 for a shelter adoption to several hundred dollars for a purebred cat. Beyond that, though, you'll have to pay for food, litter, toys, and regular medical expenses. The ASPCA estimates that in the first year of owning a cat, you will likely spend about $1,035 on it. (That amount goes down after you've bought the major equipment and had your initial medical procedures.)

5. Consider adopting a cat from an animal shelter. The cost is minimal considering what you get: a fully vaccinated, health examined, and spayed or neutered cat. Any "free" cat is ultimately going to cost you those things down the line, if you're a responsible cat owner.

Part 2

Housetraining your Cat

1. Encourage the cat to use a litter box. Most cats will prefer the litter box to other parts of the

house because of the texture of the litter. But, there are still steps you need to take to make sure you're offering the litter box as the best place to use the bathroom.

- Place the box in a quiet spot where the cat won't be bothered by people, dogs, or loud noises.

- Keep the litter box clean — scoop the litter daily, and clean the box weekly. You should also replace or refresh the litter at least once a week.

- Provide enough litter boxes for more than one cat. If you have 2 cats, you need 3 litter boxes in different areas of the home. One cat might try to intimidate a less dominate cat away from using a single box.

2. Make the litter box a comfortable place. Don't frighten or startle your cat when it's using the box, or it may form a bad association with the box and start avoiding it. Buy a large box, even if you have to spend a little money on it. Cats are more comfortable in a larger (in area, not height) box.

- Don't switch brands of litter on your cat, because cats don't like sudden change. Switching from a clay litter to a scoopable clumping type of litter or vice versa might upset the cat so much it stops using the box.

- Don't use heavily scented litters that might deter a cat from litter box use.

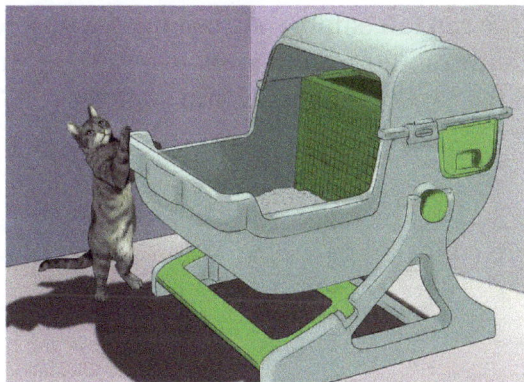

3. Take young or old cats needs into consideration. Keep in mind that kittens and older cats with arthritis or other health problems may have problems getting in and out of a box that's too tall. Use low-height boxes in an easily accessible area for kittens and cats with special needs, or buy an adjustable litter box.

4. Provide the cat with a scratching post. Scratching is a normal part of cat behavior, and there's no way you can train it out of them. If your cat still has its claws, he'll need one or two scratching posts to keep him from scratching up furniture, wood work, and so on. By providing a post, you allow the cat to indulge in normal, healthy behavior.

5. Discourage the cat from exploring forbidden surfaces. Cats are curious, and will jump on counters or other places you'd like them to stay clear of. Scat mats, a perfectly timed mist of water from a spray bottle, or even a stern "no" can correct this behavior. With time and patience, you can teach your cat to stay away from your protected areas.

- You can also use a rattle can (an empty soda can filled with a few pebbles and the opening taped over). Toss it gently on the ground to scare a cat away from forbidden surfaces. DO NOT throw the can at the cat, for that may harm your cat.

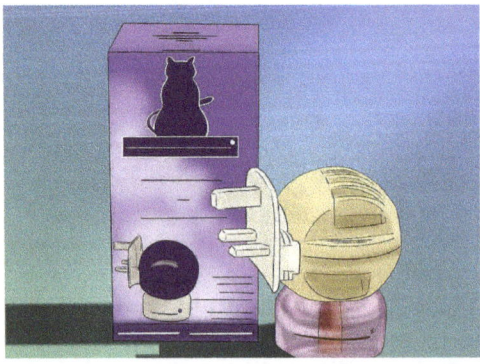

6. Consider using feline pheromone products. These products, which fill the air with calming

synthetic pheromones, come as sprays or diffusers that plug into electrical outlets. They can help resolve litter box or scratching issues, and have also been proven to calm stressed or anxious cats.

Part 3

Feeding your Cat

1. Decide what type of food to feed your cat. Cat food comes in a vast array of types: dry food, semi-moist, and canned are the common types. Dry food is easily and efficiently stored, but cats go wild for the taste of semi-moist and canned foods. The latter types can add more fluid to the cat's diet than dry foods. In general, food type comes down to owner preference.

- Occasionally, a cat with a medical condition might need one type over another. Consult your veterinarian for recommendations.

2. Choose a good brand of cat food. Like other animals, cats have some specific nutritional needs. They are "obligate carnivores," which means they need animal proteins to avoid severe health consequences. Ask your vet for suggestions about a good quality food. Cheaper products may not provide enough nutrition to keep your cat happy and healthy.

- Look for cat foods that list large amounts of animal meat like beef, chicken, turkey, or fish.

- Also look for important amino acids like taurine and arginine and fatty acids like arachidonic and linoleic acid.

- Avoid feeding your cat human foods unless you have cleared the food with your veterinarian. Some human foods can make a cat severely sick or are even toxic to cats (e.g., chocolate).

3. Follow your cat food's suggested feeding guide. In general, cats are fed according to age, weight and activity levels. They prefer to eat frequent, small meals throughout the day.

- Ask your vet for recommendations on what and how to feed your cat if you have any reservations.

4. Don't overfeed your cat. Follow your veterinarian's recommendations closely and make sure your cat gets plenty of exercise, as obesity is one of the biggest health issues facing cats today. Obese cats are more likely to develop diabetes when they approach middle age. Extra weight also contributes to arthritis, heart disease, and other health problems in cats.

Part 4

Keeping your Cat Healthy

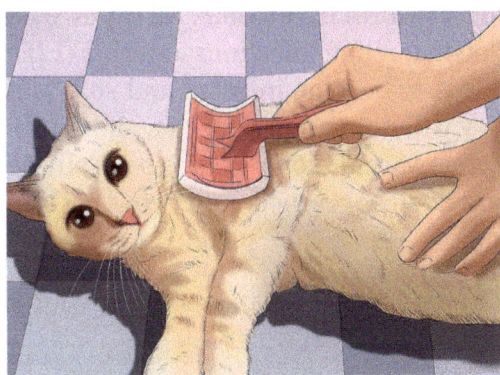

1. Brush your cat depending on it's coat needs. You may think that because cats seem to groom themselves, you don't need to brush them. But you do need to brush long-hair cats several times a week and short-hair cats weekly. This will help reduce shedding in your home and also help the cat avoid the dreaded hairballs.

- For cats that tend to shed (long-haired ones especially), use a comb that has fine strands of metal. This gets deep into the undercoat and eliminates shedding.

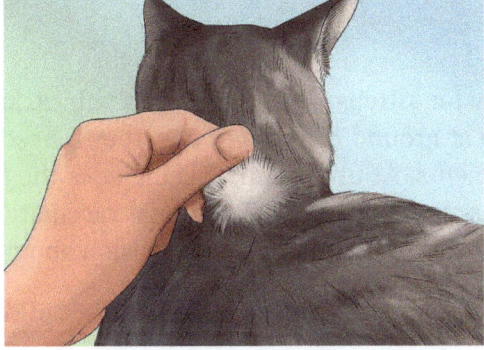

2. Check the cat for skin conditions as you brush. Be on the lookout for any fleas or other parasites, and for any unusual redness, lumps, bumps, or other skin problems. If you see anything suspicious, let your veterinarian know and ask for advice on how you should take care of it.

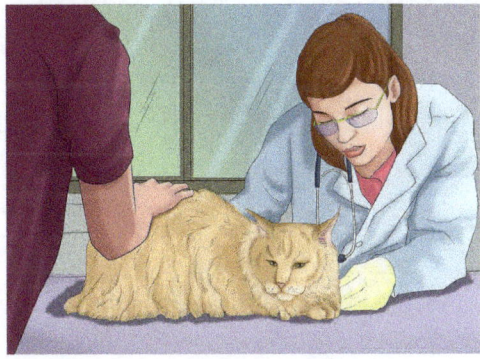

3. Schedule yearly vet visits. Just like any member of the family, a cat needs regular medical visits.

Unlike human children, cats can't let us know when they're not feeling well. They rely on their humans to take them to a veterinarian for regular medical examinations to keep them healthy. It is important that a cat sees a vet at least once a year, for a physical check-up: teeth, ears, eyes, heart, booster vaccinations, and deflea/deworm treatments. All cat owners should consider getting their pet vaccinated against the following: feline infectious enteritis (FIE), cat 'flu and feline leukaemia virus (FeLV). All can kill cats if they become infected and so it is important to protect your pet. You may also find that a cattery will not accept your pet, should you need their services, without proof of these and potentially other vaccinations. Your vet can advise exactly what vaccinations are required for your pet. If you are at all concerned about your cat's health or behaviour you should see your vet as soon as possible.

- Older cats might need to see a veterinarian twice yearly for optimal health.

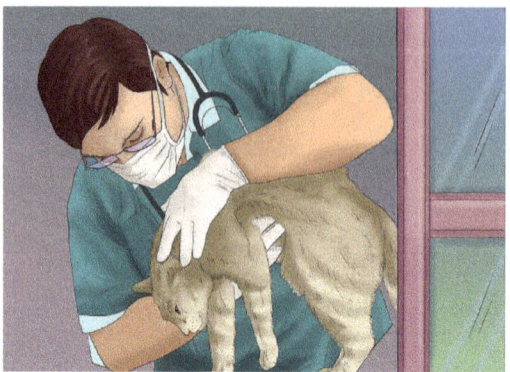

4. Visit the vet more frequently for kittens. Just like human babies, kittens need to see the vet more often than adult cats. Starting at around 8 weeks of age, they'll need 2-3 visits to have their vaccination series and worm treatments. At minimum, this includes the feline distemper vaccine and a rabies vaccine. Your vet will discuss the benefits of optional vaccinations as well. Ask about the risks of diseases like feline leukemia and make an informed decision about which vaccinations you want.

- The vet will also check the kitten for fleas and ear mites, and treat them if needed.

- Make sure the kitten gets its worm treatment. Most kittens have roundworms that can stunt growth and potentially be transmitted to humans.

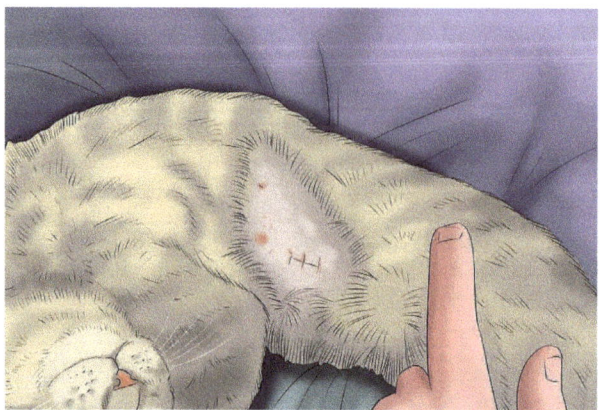

5. Get your cat spayed or neutered (or "fixed"). Spaying a female cat or neutering a male cat has

many positive benefits. It will cut down on unwanted behaviors like roaming and the tendency to spray urine. Physically, it protects against unwanted pregnancies and diseases like pyometra. The most important thing, though, is that it cuts down on the number of unwanted kittens in the world!

- Ask your vet for a recommendation on when to get kittens spayed or neutered. In general, vets recommend a range from 2-6 months.

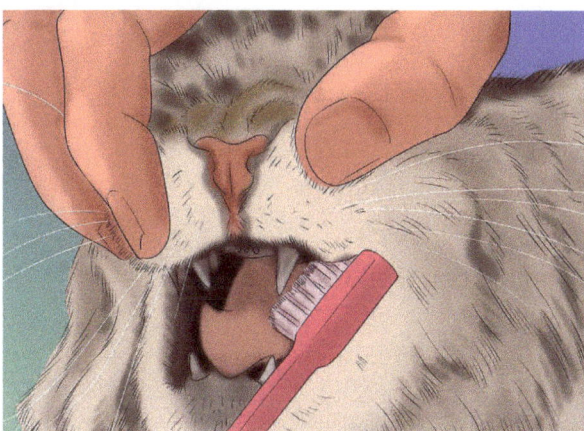

6. Get the cat used to tooth brushing. Cats can and do suffer from dental disease. To brush your cat's teeth, you need a soft-bristled toothbrush and veterinary toothpaste. *Never use human toothpaste* — too much fluoride can upset your cat's stomach, and with the high fluoride concentration in human toothpaste, too much could be toxic. Start by offering him/her a taste of the veterinary toothpaste. The next time, let him/her taste the toothpaste, and then run your finger along the gums of the upper teeth. Repeat the process with the toothbrush. Get the bristles of the brush along the gum line of the upper back teeth and angle slightly up, so the bristles get under the gum line. Work from back to front, making small circles along the gum lines. It should take you less than 30 seconds to brush your pet's teeth.

- Do not try to brush the entire mouth at first. If he/she only lets you brush the outside of her upper teeth, it's better than nothing. You're still addressing the most important area of dental disease prevention.

7. Schedule professional tooth cleaning if needed. Even with the best tooth brushing, some cats

may still need an occasional professional cleaning. While brushing reduces the plaque and buildup on the visible surfaces of the teeth it cannot get to the buildup just under the gum line. A professional cleaning also gives the vet a chance to fully examine her mouth under sedation. Some signs of dental disease include:

- Bad breath

- Loose teeth

- Discolored teeth or teeth covered in tartar

- Sensitivity or pain in the mouth

- Bleeding

- Drooling a lot or dropping food while trying to eat

- Loss of appetite or weight loss

8. Make sure your cat gets enough play time. Your cat needs interaction with you daily to keep him/her both emotionally happy and physically fit. Use cat toys, talking, and grooming as chances to spend time together. Laser pointers, balls, play mice, and feather toys are also good ways to engage your cat in play.

How to Care for a Rabbit

If you are thinking about getting a pet, you may want to consider getting a rabbit. Rabbits make excellent house pets, as they have wonderful personalities and easily adapt to a domestic lifestyle, even adjusting well to living in apartments. To stay healthy and happy, rabbits do need some special care, beginning with plenty of hay and veggies, a warm, cozy nest, and time to run and hop to their hearts' content. It's sometimes great to keep a rabbit inside at night to protect it from predators like coyotes, skunks, foxes, wolves, dogs and cats.

Part 1

Making a Home

1. Get an appropriately-sized cage. For an average-sized rabbit of 8 pounds or so, you'll need a cage that's at least four feet wide, two feet deep, and two feet tall. The bunny should be able to lay down and stretch out comfortably and still have room for food and water and a litter box.

- Outdoor hutches for rabbits can be purchased or you can build one yourself. The hutch should have room for the rabbit to nest, hop around, space for food and water and a litter box.

- Get an exercise pen to provide extra space for the rabbit to move around.

- Big bunnies will need larger accommodations. The rabbit needs to be able to move around and lay down freely. Make sure to have a large enough cage so that your rabbit can play!

2. Get the right type of cage. Look for a cage with a solid bottom and sides made out of wire designed for rabbits. Think of this as the "den" for the rabbit to sleep in and a source of food and

water. The plan should be that the bunny spends 8-12 hours or so outside of the cage in an exercise pen or a room for bunny-safe exploration.

- If you find a cage with a wire bottom, put a solid wood plank inside to line the bottom. Wire cage bottoms can hurt rabbits' feet.

- An outdoor hutch should be sturdy and provide protection from the weather and predators. You can buy or build a hutch. You will need to make sure the rabbits are protected from predators and the elements.

- Do not house your rabbit outdoors in a hutch all by itself. Rabbits are highly social animals, so get a companion rabbit when they are both young and have the rabbits spayed or neutered.

3. Line the cage with hay or soft wood shavings, such as those made of pine bedding is very dangerous for all rodents DO NOT GET PINE BEDDING instead get aspen bedding. There are also some specialty beddings made of recycled wood pulp that work well. Rabbits like to make cozy nests, so fill the bottom of the cage with soft natural material to keep them comfortable.

- Hay, in addition to being great bedding, is the most important part of a rabbits diet, so make sure you choose the right hay for your rabbit. Timothy or grass hays are appropriate for rabbits. avoid alfalfa hay(only if your rabbit is over six months old) as it is too high in calories, protein and calcium for long term feeding for all adult rabbits.

4. Place the cage in a rabbit-proof area. You'll want to be able to let your bunny out to hop around,

so place the cage in a room that you don't mind sharing and that is safe for the bunny. For instance, remove all electrical cords, small objects, and furniture of value from the room and avoid having chemicals or plants that may harm the rabbit in the room.

- Rabbits like to chew cords but you can buy cord protectors from hardware stores to stop your rabbit from chewing them.

- Use a baby gate or exercise pen for dogs to prevent full access to the house to avoid damage to the furnishings and the bunny.

5. Provide a litter box. Rabbits will naturally use the same spot as a "restroom" over and over, usually one corner of the cage. Line a small litter box (available at pet stores) with newspaper, then fill it with hay, or litter made specifically for rabbits, and place it in the rabbit's preferred corner.

- Consider putting a second litter box in the rabbit's play area.

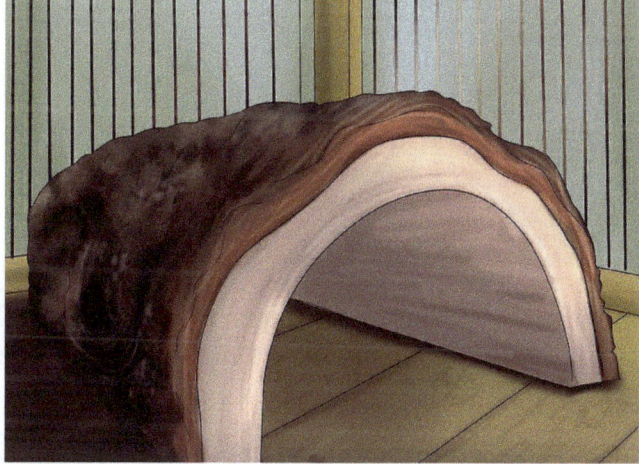

6. Provide a hiding place in your rabbit's cage. Rabbits are burrowing prey animals, so providing hiding places, like logs or cardboard boxes, is good for their well-being. One or two per rabbit, depending on how much space you have, will give the rabbits plenty of room to huddle.

7. Provide cardboard boxes for the rabbit play in, hide in and chew on. Rabbits adore chewing, and it keeps their teeth healthy. If you don't provide rabbit chews as snacks, it may chew on your furniture or other items you have lying around.

- Make sure your rabbit always has something safe to chew on. This will wear down its teeth and prevent injury.

Part 2

Providing Food, Snacks and Water

1. Put out unlimited grass hay. This is the main component of a rabbit's diet and so it should be available at all times. Timothy, oat, and brome hay are good choices. Put it out on a daily basis in a clean area of the rabbit's cage.

- For young growing rabbits (up to 7 months) or pregnant or lactating rabbits, feed alfalfa hay and pellets to provide extra calories needed for these life stages.

- Dried ready grass hay is available from pet shops and feed stores or you can grow a tray of grass specially for the rabbit.

2. Give the rabbit a dish of rabbit alfalfa or timothy hay pellets. These contain protein and fiber, essential for growing bunnies. Adult rabbits should get 1/8 cup for every 5 pounds of body weight.

- Rabbits are herbivores and even hay and vegetables can make them gain weight. Pellets are more concentrated energy than hay and should be fed sparingly.

- Remember that your rabbit can't live on pellets alone. It is very important for the rabbit's digestive tract to have long stem indigestible fiber in the form of Timothy or grass hay to prevent hairballs (trichobezoars) and to keep its digestive system happy and healthy. Chewing on long stem fiber also helps to wear down the rabbit's continuously growing (hypsodont) teeth and prevent dental problems.

- Baby rabbits can have as many alfalfa pellets as they want until they are 6-7 months of age.

3. Offer plenty of vegetables. Rabbits are famous for loving carrots, but these should only be given occasionally, as they have a high sugar content. Wash the veggies completely and, if possible, feed organic greens.

- Provide leafy greens like spinach as well as collards and turnip greens. In addition mustard greens, cilantro/parsley, watercress, celery, and dandelion leaves are good vegetables for your rabbit.

- Two cups of vegetables a day is a good amount for most adult rabbits.

- Introduce greens a little at a time to avoid digestive upset. Younger rabbits, 12 weeks an older, you can add in one veggie a week, about a half an ounce at a time to avoid disrupting the cecum.

- You can also feed your rabbit fruits like apples, blueberries, strawberries and bananas as special treats. Fruit is high in sugar, and should be fed sparingly, about 1 to 2 ounces per 6 pounds of body weight.

4. Avoid giving your rabbit foods that are bad for it. Some vegetables aren't good for rabbits, including corn, iceberg lettuce, tomatoes, cabbage, beans, peas, potatoes, beets, onions, kale and rhubarb. Also avoid feeding the rabbit with bamboo, seeds, grains, and any type of meat.

- Human foods such as bread, chocolate, candy, dairy, and anything cooked should not be given to rabbits.

- Do not give your bunny light lettuce (such as iceberg). It may kill them by causing diarrhea and digestive upset of the good bacteria in the gut. Romaine is best, but make sure it's organic if possible, and wash it before offering it to your rabbit.

- Never give rabbits grass cuttings, as this will cause serious health problems. You can allow a rabbit to eat grass that has not been sprayed with herbicides or pesticides and let the bunny choose what to eat on the lawn. However, avoid cut grass that has been heated and crushed by the mower. The process of cutting it will hasten the fermentation process and can lead to bunny digestive problems.

5. Provide plenty of clean water. Fresh water must always be available and changed daily. You can put

it in a bowl or in a bottle of the sort used to feed hamsters, but rabbit size, although a bowl of water can be easily spilled. Make sure it never runs out and clean it out frequently to prevent contamination.

- Make sure, if using a water bottle, that it is working properly and is not stuck open or closed.

Part 3

Giving the Rabbit Exercise and Play Time

1. Introduce yourself to a new rabbit slowly. When you first get a rabbit leave it in its cage or hutch so it can get used to its home. Don't approach it straight away and start playing with it, as it hasn't really settled in yet and doesn't really know you and trust you yet.

- Approach a new rabbit slowly and calmly so the rabbit doesn't get scared. Rabbits get scared very easy, can't see very well, so you should speak before approaching.

2. Let the rabbit out for several hours (6 to 8, if you can) per day. Rabbits love to hop and run around, and to stay healthy they need the opportunity to do so for several hours every single day. You can play with your bunny or leave it to enjoy itself on its own (but keeping an eye on it), but don't neglect this important element of rabbit care.

- Make sure your rabbit is either fenced in a pen that is at least 1 foot (0.3 m) in the ground and 3 feet (0.9 m) out of the ground, or on a rabbit harness and leash.

- If you'd like to play with the bunny outside, make sure you're in a fenced-in area, and never leave it unattended.

- Keep cats, dogs, and predatory birds away from the bunny at all times.

3. Give the bunny plenty of toys. They like to chew up cardboard boxes and old phone books. You can also try playing with your bunny by tossing a small ball or stuffed toy.

4. Pick up the rabbit carefully. Rabbits have fragile bodies and must be handled with care. Put a hand under its rear and front area and hold it close to your body. Never pick up a rabbit by his ears.

- Most rabbits enjoy being petted.

- Don't handle the rabbit roughly or pet it when it is clearly not enjoying it. Rabbits get stressed out easily when they aren't comfortable.

5. Take time to bond. Bonding with your rabbits can be slightly difficult to begin with, as they like being given treats and a little scratch behind the ears occasionally, but much to people's surprise, a lot of the time they enjoy being picked up less. This is because (especially when you first get them) they don't like being taken out of their comfort zone and this can leave them feeling exposed. Don't be disheartened if at the beginning they bite and scratch furiously every time you try. It is like this for virtually every new rabbit owner. Remember to be gentle and calm, and don't get angry at yourself or the rabbit. Keep working at it, when you do it successfully, give them a small treat such as apple to let them know they have done a good job.

- When you have bonded with your rabbits, interact with them as much as possible. This helps to build a happy and great relationship which is very rewarding as rabbits are curious and playful animals, and will give out as much love as they get back.

Part 4

Keeping More than One Rabbit

1. Consider getting several rabbits at the same time. Rabbits are social animals and they enjoy playing with other members of their species. Caring for two bunnies isn't much harder than caring for one, so you might want to invest in a second pet so they'll both be happy.

- Make sure the bunnies are spayed or neutered, especially if you're housing them in the same cage.

- Be sure to get one that is a good fit with the rabbit you already have.

- If you think you want more than one rabbit, get litter-mates at the same time so they are the same age and similar size. Have the bunnies spayed or neutered right away so you don't have unwanted litters and you prevent some hormonally driven behavior issues.

2. Introduce new rabbits to an established household gradually. You will need to introduce them slowly to prevent fighting. Rabbits can be territorial. A male and female or two females will likely be easier matches than two males, unless they are babies.

- Have the rabbits in cages far apart on neutral ground for a few days and watch what they do. If they are thumping and agitated, place the rabbits further apart or in separate rooms for a few more days and then bring them back in eyesight. This would be a good time, when introducing them, to have yummy veggies to distract the rabbits but also increase the positive association of the presence of the other rabbit.

- Gradually decrease the distance between the cages until they are next to each other, but still safe from "attack." As long as they are peacefully co-existing in cages next to each other, continue this arrangement for at least a week.

- Then, you can place them in exercise pens with a barrier between them and, if all is okay, allow the rabbits to meet without a barrier, under supervision for a short period of time. Place yummy greens in there, two to three piles, to reinforce all is good. When rabbits are laying down together or grooming each other, bunny life is good.

Part 5

Keeping your Rabbit Healthy

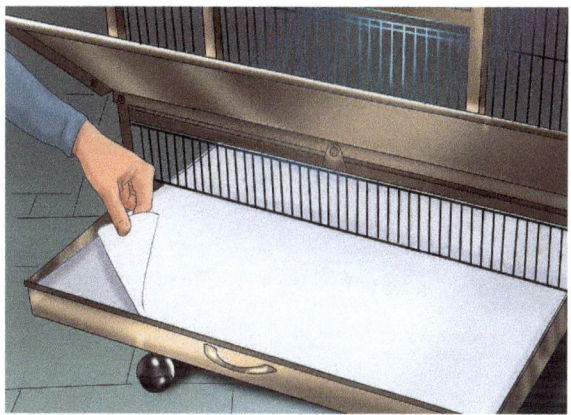

1. Clean the cage every week. Make sure the bunny is under supervision while you work. Empty the dirty hay or shavings from the cage, wash it with hot, soapy water, rinse it thoroughly, and let it dry. Fill it with clean hay or shavings.

- You should wash out the water dish or bottle every day.

- The litter box needs to be changed out every day, and thoroughly disinfected every week or so with a 10% bleach or 10% white vinegar solution. Rinse well and allow to dry. If the litter box is plastic or metal, you can also place it in the dishwasher.

- Have more than one litter box, so that you can switch a clean one while the other box is dirty or in the process of being cleaned.

- Rabbit urine is very alkaline and crystals can build up on the surface of the litter box and require the use of a descaling solution.

2. Keep the temperature right for your rabbit. Optimum temperature for rabbits is 61 to 72ºF. If your rabbit is outside, provide plenty of shade and, if it gets really hot, bring them indoors to air conditioning or place frozen water bottles in the hutch to help the rabbit keep cool. Rabbits can die of heat stroke.

- The rabbit's ears are really the main temperature control part of their bodies.

- If they were in the wild, the rabbit would go underground where it is cool to get out of the heat.

3. Brush the rabbit. Bathing isn't necessary, but you can use a soft-bristled brush to carefully remove hair every day or two. If you have two rabbits, you may notice them grooming each other.

- Rabbit shampoo can be purchased if your rabbit is extremely dirty. Rabbits generally do not need to be bathed unless they get very dirty and are not able to groom themselves properly.

- Discuss bathing frequency with your veterinarian, but in general, bathing a rabbit every 1-2 months, if at all, is plenty.

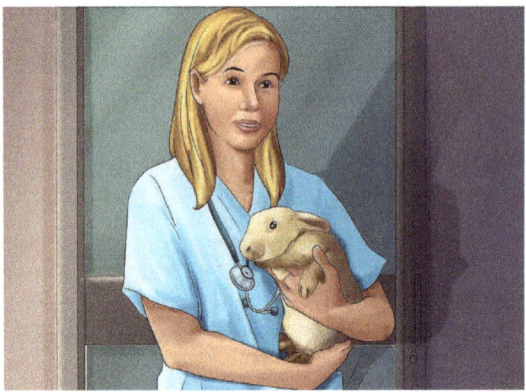

4. Take the rabbit to the veterinarian at least once a year. Rabbits need annual checkups to make sure they're healthy. Many veterinarians who treat cats and dogs do not have expertise in treating bunnies, so you may need to find a vet who treats "exotic" animals.

- Depending on where you live, your veterinarian may recommend vaccination for certain diseases like Myxomatosis if you live in the United Kingdom. In the United States, Myxomatosis vaccination is not currently recommended.

- Your veterinarian will do an examination and discuss their findings and make recommendations based on your rabbit's current condition. Managing healthy dentition in rabbits may require anesthesia to fully examine the teeth and address any sharp points discovered on the back teeth (premolars and molars).

5. Learn how to read rabbit body language. Knowing how your rabbit is feeling is extremely important if you want your bunny to be happy and healthy.

- If a rabbit's ears are flat on its back, its eyes are bulging and it body is tense and hunched up, it is scared. If a rabbit is really terrified, it may be trembling and breathing heavily.

- If a rabbit is very relaxed chilled out, it will be laying stretched out with its front paws in front of it, or it may have all its paws tucked beneath its body. It may also be laying on its side. Its ears may be flat on its back.

- Sometimes, when a rabbit is extremely happy and excited, it will jump into the air and flick its body. This is called a binky. Many rabbits will run around very quickly before binkying. Sometimes, if a rabbit is feeling lazy, it won't do a proper binky, but will remain on the ground and do a sort of shuddery-flick.

How to Take Care of your Fish

Fish come in all different shapes and sizes. You name it: spikes, tails. Fish are cool. But how do you look after them? All those water chemicals, live food, and business about putting two fish in the same tank sounds scary. However, don't sweat it... just read this guide! It contains all the information you need on taking care of those first fins.

Steps

1. Decide whether you want Tropical or Coldwater fish. Coldwater fish include goldfish and

minnows. There are many types of tropical fish, from angelfish to corydoras catfish. Coldwater fish are usually a little more hardy, and will survive those first few mistakes, but they need more room.

- Start off with inexpensive fish, even if you can afford expensive ones. Inexpensive ones are inexpensive because they are very successful in their natural environments or so comfortable in captivity that they even breed regularly and, in either case, do not die easily on their way to and in pet stores.

- Do not start out with saltwater fish. They require techniques and understanding that are much more complex. Plus, the water you'll have to work with and that may leak is messy, slowly corrosive to metal, and conductive. If you believe you want a saltwater tank, get a medium sized tropical fish tank with some plants and see if you can keep that in perfect order first for a year or so.

2. Decide what kind and how many fish you want.

- Research before putting species together. Some fish are compatible, others aren't. One might speculate that fish would enjoy some activity in their lives, so don't get just one. (The fish need not be the same species; for some territorial fish, it is best that it isn't. An armored catfish can be a good "companion" for such a beast.)

- Make sure you can provide any specialized care the fish need. For example, different fish need different foods, and some fish require more frequent maintenance than others. Owning fish is a big responsibility.

- Some fish are perfectly happy with flakes and can be fed with an automatic feeder, which makes it possible to leave the tank unattended for a week or two (assuming the fish are small so the water doesn't need very frequent changing).

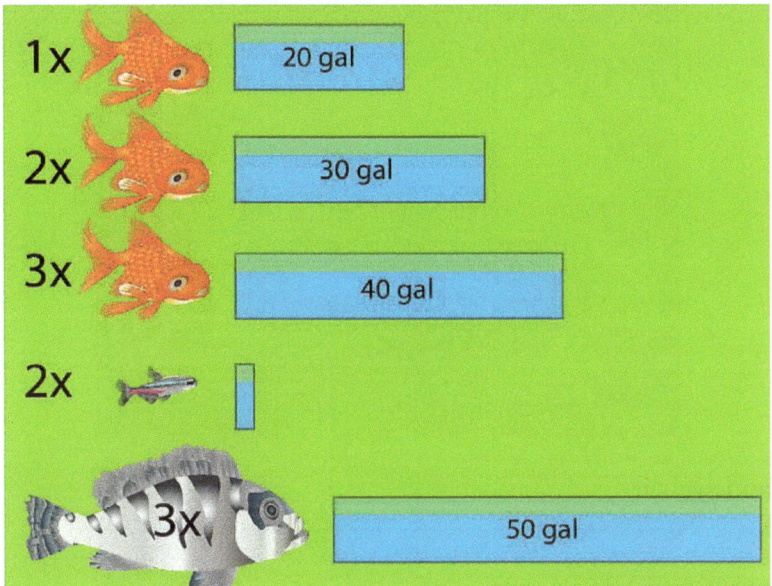

3. Get an appropriately sized tank. Look up the minimum tank size for each fish.

- For goldfish, buy a tank with 20 gallons (75.7 L) for the first goldfish, and 10 gallons (37.9 L) for each additional goldfish.

- For freshwater fish, forget about one gallon per inch of adult fish. would you keep a 50 inch (127.0 cm) fish in a 50 gallon (189.3 L) tank?

- Bigger is better. Even if the fish looks small, it will thrive in a bigger tank.

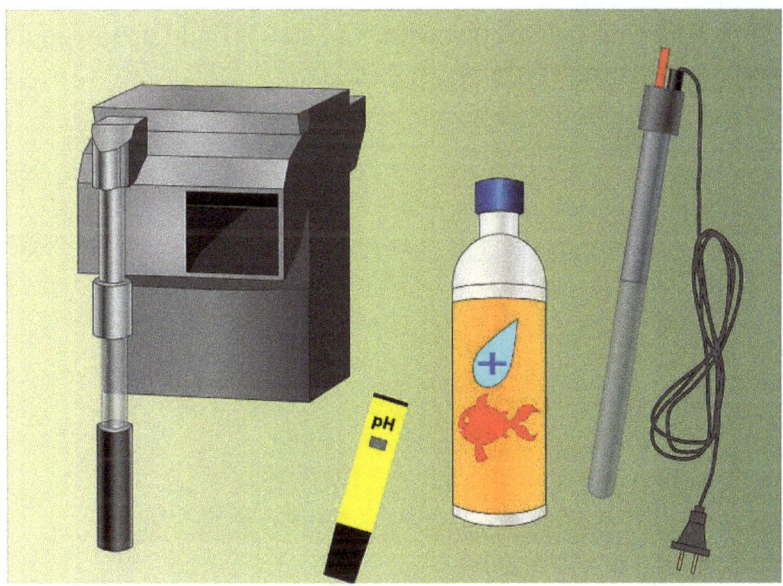

4. Make sure you have all the proper equipment- filters, heaters (for tropical fish), water conditioner, test kit, etc.

5. Set up the tank and cycle it.

6. Put your fish in. Only add a few fish to start with, and slowly build up the population. Adding too many fish at once can overload your filtration system.

7. Perform partial water changes weekly. 20-30% is a good amount. To do a water change, get a gravel vacuum and siphon out any waste in the substrate. This will pull out water at the same time. Replace the water with water from your tap, but remember to treat it with a water conditioner.

8. Test the water regularly. Make sure you have 0 ammonia, 0 nitrite, and under 40 nitrate.

9. Feed your fish two or three times a day.

10. Monitor your fish. While they eat, sit and observe them. Check for anything strange: changing color, falling off fins, damaged tails, etc. Also, make sure all your fish are getting along.

11. Try not to stress out your fish. This includes putting your hand in the tank when you don't need to, touching them, or jumping near the tank. Try not to make too much unnecessary noise.

How to Care for a Bird

Extremely social by nature, birds need company, nurturing and constant interaction. Birds are wonderful both as pets and as visitors to the garden. If you're considering bird ownership, the care requirements include providing good housing, nutritious food and keeping an eye on the bird's health. You'll also need to provide plenty of enrichment and interaction, to keep your pet bird happy and alert. Or, if what you're doing is encouraging birds to your yard to feed, you'll still need to know some care basics to make their visits safer and more enjoyable. This article is intended to give you an overview on general bird care and the things that it pays to think about as either a bird owner or provider of bed-and-breakfast-for-the-birds.

Part 1

Choosing a Bird as a Pet

1. Choose the bird species with care. Not all bird species are appropriate as pets and not all bird

temperaments or care needs will suit what you're able to provide. It is very important to learn as much as you can about the species of birds that interest you, well before deciding which bird you will choose. The bird must match your lifestyle, interests and ability to take good care of it for the time it lives (which can a very long time for some birds). You must be willing to interact with the bird and provide daily interaction, as well as supervising time outside of the cage, where possible.

- Don't buy a bird on impulse. You need the time to research the bird's needs and longevity before bringing one home. Check out books on birds or read online articles on bird species and specific bird requirements, to learn more about the different types of bird species.

2. Familiarize yourself with the most common species of birds owned as pets. Parrots, cockatiels and cockatoos, or parakeets tend to be some of the most popular types of birds owned as pets. Other good pet species include: Canaries, finches, lovebirds, doves and pigeons. The more exotic or less common the bird type, the more consideration you need to give as to whether it is one you can provide appropriate care for.

3. Consider the bird's longevity. Some birds, such as parrots, live long lives, so this should be a consideration when purchasing a parrot. Arrangements may have to be made to care for parrot after the owner dies; in some cases, you might consider taking on the responsibility of caring for a bird in such a predicament rather than getting a young one.

4. If getting more than one bird, consider the appropriate housing arrangements. Some birds will be able to share housing, while others might not get along; indeed, "cage mate trauma" is commonplace and can depend on such issues as personalities, size differences, gender and species. Although it will depend on the species, you might be able to house two boys or two girls or a boy and girl. If they fight, you'll need to separate them. Do plenty of research beforehand and ask questions of the breeder or retailer; you could even talk to bird keepers at your local zoo or wildlife refuge for advice.

- There are often special methods needed for introducing a new bird to a cage with an existing bird. Talk to a veterinarian or bird expert for advice.

Part 2

Housing a Bird

1. Purchase the right kind of cage for housing the bird. The cage required will vary by type of bird; as such, be guided by the species you're choosing. That said, some fairly standard requirements include:

- The cage size should be sufficient for the bird to stretch its wings from side to side. For some birds, being able to fly short distances within the cage may be an important part of ensuring it has a healthy living space. At a minimum, large birds should only be housed in a cage that is one and a half times the height of the bird's wingspan (depth, width and height).

- The cage bars should not be too small; the bird's talons might get caught on or in them if the bar wires or lengths are too small. Equally, the bars should not be so large that the head of the bird could get trapped or the bird could squeeze through and escape.

- The bigger the space in the cage, the better. Although bird cages that are bigger tend to be harder to clean and are more expensive, if you are not in the house often and/or don't have time to take the bird out for exercise, space in their cage is critical. Small cages tend to lead to behavior problems.

2. Consider the cage shape. A simple rectangle cage is always the best. Circle cages are bad for the bird. There is hardly any space for the bird, and no corners to feel safe in. Moreover, the circle tends to cause the bird to twist its head; the bird can go insane from the constant turning and turning.

- Never buy guillotine-styled doors, since they are easier to escape and dangerous if the bird attempts to escape and gets its head caught under the door.

3. Ensure that the space is more than adequate if housing more than one bird. Never house more

than one bird in a small cage. Birds need space to retreat, forage, fly and be apart from other birds, so the more birds being kept, the larger the cage must be. Aviaries (large cages that are akin to small sheds) are more appropriate for keeping several birds at the same time.

- If keeping different species of birds, you'll need to be sure that they're compatible when placed together.

4. Ensure that placement of the cage is somewhere warm and comfortable. The placement of the cage will be dependent on the climate you live in. If you have severe winters, with temperatures below zero, snow, etc., it is not appropriate to keep the birds outdoors during winter. If you live in a more temperate to warm climate, outdoor aviaries might be more appropriate than an indoor cage. Again, you'll need to research the needs of the individual birds, the temperature requirements and assess these needs against the typical climate in your area.

- In some cases, a combination of an indoor/outdoor cage arrangement might provide the optimal housing arrangements for your birds. This could vary between seasons or weather patterns, or it could be a day and night arrangement.

- Birds in hanging cages can often be transported outdoors to hang under a porch or similar place for daytime fresh air. Always remember to bring the bird back in before cool evening breezes and night air arrive.

- See the "Bird hygiene and health" section below for signs of overheating or chilling in birds.

- Location of the bird's cage will also be affected by the bird's personality. While a very social bird might love being the center of attention and seeing constant human traffic, a more nervous bird might be happier kept somewhere quieter and away from hustle and bustle (but still being able to interact with the family).

- Avoid placing a cage in front of a window permanently. The bird will be on the constant lookout for "enemies", which can cause it to feel nervous. Putting a cage against a wall can give the bird a break from worrying about predators.

5. Place some old magazines/unneeded papers on the bottom of the cage. This makes cleaning much easier, and the papers can be disposed of with ease, then fresh ones placed straight down for the next day's use. Keep a supply handy from your junk mail and newspaper reads.

Part 3

Bringing the Bird Home

1. Transport the bird in a proper carrying container. This should be a hard-sided carrier, such as a cat cage or a cage recommended by the breeder or store. Secure it well in the car, so that it will not move about during the journey home. A towel can be thrown over the cage to provide privacy but be sure there is adequate air flow for the bird to keep cool and breathe well.

2. When you first bring the bird home, leave it for a day to get used to its environment. This also applies when moving the cage to another part of the house if it's still relatively young.

Allowing for a settling-in time will help the bird grow accustomed to its environment in its own way, without feeling threatened by looming humans. However, be sure to leave it adequate food and water.

Part 4

Feeding a Bird

1. Identify the exact foods needed by the species of bird you're caring for. Some birds thrive on specific types of food only, while other birds may be able to have a more generalized diet. Since precise dietary requirements are dependent on the species, you are advised to do careful reading on this topic in relation to the bird species you're choosing. Some general feeding observations include:

- Ensure that you have correct feed for the species of bird. You must find the correct food for your bird, as some birds are picky, while others have very strict dietary requirements. Usually the bag/can of food will have a label telling you which bird it is for. If you don't know what the best food choices are, ask the breeder, the retailer or leave a question on a specialized forum of people who care for this species of bird.

- You may need to put a bit of grit (sand or small rocks) in a bowl; some passerine birds need this to assist crushing seeds in the crop (chest area). However, not all birds need this grit, and if they eat too much, it can create a blockage. Finches and canaries tend to find a little grit necessary, but don't give it to budgies, cockatiels or parrots.

- Millet is a treat; never feed too much of it to birds. It is best used as a treat during training.

- Bird pellets, crumbles or nuggets can be a good way of ensuring adequate nutrition for your bird; since these tend to combine all manner of needed seeds, vegetables, fruits and grains, there is less likelihood of the bird being picky and favoring only one food, thus the bird is more likely to eat a nutritionally balanced diet.

- Give your feathered friends the same kinds of fresh and healthy fruit and vegetables you enjoy, minus the dressings. This adds greens and variety to their diet. A mixture or variety of foods is both healthy and fun for birds.

- Feed new seed daily; always empty out the eaten shells the same day too, as this keeps the seed fresh and clean.

- If the bird you have requires nectar, this is a highly specialized diet and you must learn as much as possible about it *before* obtaining the bird.

2. Know what birds should not be fed. There are some foods that are not suitable for many species of birds. For example, don't feed the bird any alcohol, chocolate or avocado. Each of these contain chemical components that can be toxic for the bird.

3. Provide constant fresh water. There should be a water dish provided; fill this daily with average temperature water. The water feeder should be checked daily to ensure that it is working properly and you must be absolutely sure that the bird knows how to use it. Change water daily to ensure that it is always fresh.

- Have fresh dripping water if possible; it prevents fecal matter from ending up in the drinking tray.

- Dehydration can occur very quickly in birds, within 1 to 2 days without access to water.

4. Keep the feeding arrangements sanitary. Water and food cups should be located up high out of the way of any branches above them since birds often drop feces into their food, which isn't sanitary.

5. Try feeding the bird regularly at about the same time each day. This could be when you eat, or maybe earlier. However, choose a time and try to stick to it, so that the bird knows when to expect its food. If you want to stick to the natural feeding time of birds, feed approximately half an hour after sunrise and just before sunset. During the day, small fruit and vegetable snacks can be left in the cage.

- Once again, know your bird. Smaller birds with a higher metabolism may need to be fed more often.

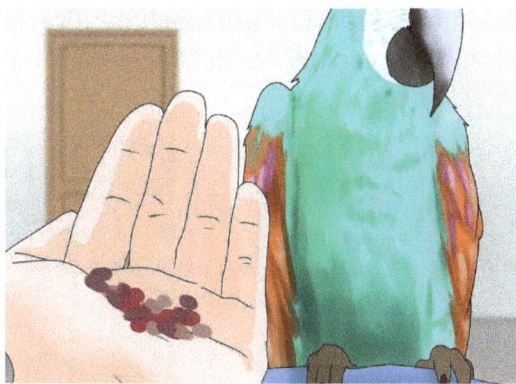

6. Make feeding interesting for the bird. You can make the eating experience more enjoyable for your bird by making eating time an interactive time too. For example, encourage your bird to eat a piece of food at a time, straight from your hand. Or, encourage your talking bird sing and talk for its food.

Part 5

Enriching your Bird's Life

1. Add enrichment material to the bird's cage to ensure that it is entertained and challenged. Birds are smart and they need to do enriching things to keep themselves occupied and to stay mentally stimulated.

2. Start off with at least four toys that are varied and interesting. Make sure they are bird-safe and that toes or beaks cannot get caught in any parts of the toys.

- Items that are not safe on toys used for birds include: Frayed ropes (could entangle bird feet and beaks); wire (might impale the bird); "jingle-bell" type bells (the bird's feet might get stuck in the small cracks).

3. Don't use the same toys over and over again. Change it up a bit! Birds can get bored with the same toys, day in and day out. Just like us, they enjoy variety and new things. By buying new toys, you increase their enjoyment and reduce the chances of feather plucking and other boredom-stimulated behaviors.

- Aim to have differently shaped and textured perches for the bird's feet. Include some wooden perches, and some natural tree branches for variety. This helps "file" the bird's beak and nails, so there is less work for you. Just be sure to scrub natural wood thoroughly before use, and do not use any cleaning products because many of these contain ingredients can be toxic to birds.

4. Place food and enrichment items in multiple places around the cage on a daily basis. This will fulfill the bird's need to move about in search of food. You can also weave food into the bars of the cage, hide food inside a toy or an enrichment device and hang food from the top or sides of the cage. All of these will help to satisfy the bird's foraging instinct and is a form of mental stimulation.

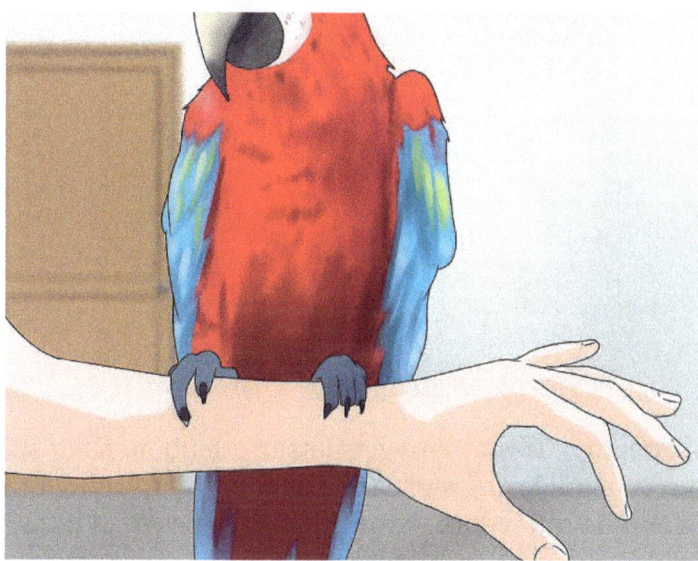

5. Get the bird used to being handled. Regularly hold and pet the bird. The more often this is done, the more excited the bird will be to see you and will likely greet you with whistles, chirps and bird talk. It also makes it easier to get your bird for health checks and for it to be reassured by your presence.

6. Ensure that the bird gets daily exercise. Daily exercise is recommended for all birds that are tame and can be handled safely. If you have a finch or other bird that is not meant to be handled, this is not an issue. But if you have a bird that you wish to handle, is living in a small cage, or just needs more exercise, be sure to include exercise for the bird on a regular basis. Just remember not to do this in a dangerous room, such as the kitchen, where a hot pot could be on.

- Birds don't enjoy being cooped up all day. If you can release the bird from its cage regularly, it will be all the happier for this. This is an absolute must if you want to have a healthy relationship with your bird; birds can suffer a lot being trapped in cages all of the time, considering birds normally fly great distances in their natural environment.

7. Give the bird lots of attention. If your bird gets lots of attention, he or she will be happier as a whole and may even prove more loving and caring as a pet than without the attention. In some cases, a good level of attention can reduce shyness in some species of birds, as familiarity breeds reassurance.

- Talk to your bird as it rides around the house with you. This is especially important during the first couple of years toget her. Birds are fast learners and will surprise you with their range of sound effects. For example, some birds will perfectly mimic the sound of water going down the drain while you wash the dishes, perhaps even mimicking the sound of you rubbing a cleaning rag over the stove, table and counter tops. Some birds can imitate the sound of appliances, such as an electric mixer, when it sees you take it out to make cakes or a smoothie.

- Play music together. For example, your bird might learn to sing sweetly when you play the piano or other instrument. What a genius your bird is!

Part 6

Taking care of Bird Hygiene and Health

1. Provide water in a large enough container for self-cleansing. Birds do not need to be cleaned as often as a dog; most likely the bird will clean itself in its water bowl, provided the bowl is large enough for it to use as a bath. Also, birds bathe to keep cool in warmer weather, so be sure to provide water for washing in when the temperature is on the warmer side.

- In hot weather, put the bird outside, either in its cage or on a perch (only have it out of its cage if its wings are clipped, so that it can't fly away). Squirt the bird with water from a spray bottle. Birds love the cooling sensation.

- If it's cold outside, you can buy a perch that mounts to your shower wall by suction cups and give the bird a shower indoors. Many birds absolutely love this!

- Provide a cuttlefish for the bird to scrape its beak against and sharpen.

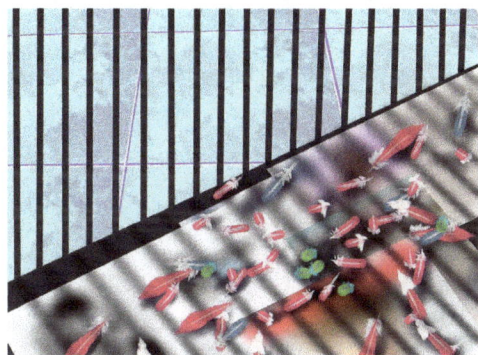

2. Keep the cage properly and regularly cleaned. A clean cage reduces the changes for bacterial, fungal or viral infections from occurring in your bird. Regular removal of bird droppings is very important for maintaining good bird health. Moreover, a bird living in a clean environment tends to be a more active and happy bird than one living in filth. If this is something you're not prepared to deal with on a daily basis, then a bird is not the right pet for you.

- Change the bedding regularly.

- Remove droppings from perches/toys.

- Remove uneaten food that has been sitting around on the base of the cage.

- If your bird is molting (this is common with parrots, for example), there will be a need to vacuum up the molted feathers daily; this tends to occur when there is a warmer spell, or when the temperature goes over 10°F.

- Only clean with basic, non-toxic cleaning supplies. Birds are easily poisoned, so find out if a product is safe for birds *before* using it.

3. Find out whether your bird's wing feathers need regular trimming. In some birds, such as parrots, this is essential to prevent serious or fatal flight accidents in the indoor or caged environment.

Talk to your veterinarian about this requirement for your bird and find someone qualified to do it, should it need doing. Trimming is aimed at restricting, not preventing flight, and only the primary flight feathers are the subject of a trimming, so the trimmer must know what to do.

- Toenails may also need trimming, especially on larger adult birds. Usually toenails are not trimmed on baby or small birds, as they need them to stay on the perches, but adult parrots, for example, should be trimmed. Ask your veterinarian to explain how to do this safely, as if you don't know, you can damage the bird and cause bleeding.

4. Know the signs of a bird that is either too hot or too cold. Most birds exhibit similar symptoms for being overheated or too cold and you must attend to fixing either situation as quickly as possible, or there is a risk of the bird dying. The things to watch for include:

- An overheated bird: The feet will feel hot to touch, the bird may be panting (a rapid breathing rate), fluttering from the throat, red nares (nasal openings) and hot breath. All of these signs signal an emergency situation and you must contact the vet immediately.

- A freezing bird: The bird will hunch in, using its feathers to covers its feet and it will fluff out its feathers. Check for drafts, move the bird away from a cold room or area, and place the bird in a warmer spot. Windows can be a source of cold air during the winter months.

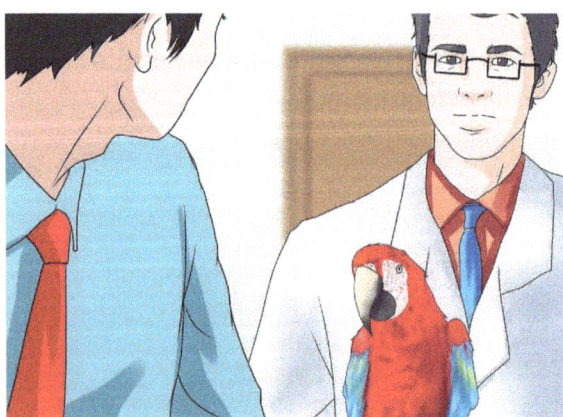

5. Find a vet who is qualified to work with birds. Get your bird checked upon purchase and then regularly afterwards (at least once a year, or as advised by your veterinarian). Should the bird fall ill, this vet will be your first port of call for the best of care.

- Do not wait when a bird gets sick. Birds can get even sicker very quickly; the sooner that the vet can see the bird, the better.

Part 7

Training Birds

1. Put effort into training your bird. In this way, you can teach it to come out of its cage and be sensible. This will give it much more freedom to enjoy flying around than remaining cooped up inside of its cage all day long. Training is a form of interaction and it plays a vital role in curbing abnormal behaviors.

- Without training, birds can end up biting, screaming, feather plucking and forming phobias. Hence, this is a very important part of keeping the bird happy and well-adjusted.

- If the bird is very well trained, then you might even be able to take it into your backyard or someplace else which is outdoors, to give the bird a breath of fresh air, and so that it can get to know the place better. You'll need to be absolutely certain it is willing to return to you though.

- Never train a bird to perch on your shoulder. This gives it easy access to pecking your eyes and face. Given the bird is at your height, it will be much harder to control.

2. When training the bird outside of its housing, check the safety of the room. Ensure that the room

the bird is contained in is safe. This includes closing blinds, rolling up cords, closing toilet seats, ensuring that hot radiators are turned off and checking that open fireplaces are closed off. (This also goes for simply allowing the bird to fly around in an enclosed space.)

- Most birds need outside-of-cage time. This time must always be supervised and the space must always be safe.

3. If training a bird to talk, be sure it is a bird that will talk before trying. Even then, birds have different personalities, so don't expect it to talk or get used to you quickly. It will learn in its own time. Be ready for a sometimes moody and sometimes fun bird; the bird doesn't see its mood changes as abnormal, but it helps for you to accept that just as with humans, the bird's level of interest in being responsive and interactive varies over time.

4. If you plan on getting two birds, separate them at first and hand-train alone. After you've fully trained them both, allow them to interact.

Part 8

Caring for Wild Birds

1. Encourage birds to your garden. Find ways to attract birds to the garden, including:

- Growing the approprping your pets away from all the areas that the birds frequent.

2. If you wish to help nesting birds, you might like to encourage them to use your yard as a nesting space. Even if you haven't provided nesting spaces, and birds are nesting in your yard, you can still be helpful by monitoring their progress and helping if needed. Some things you might like to do help wild birds breed in your yard include:

- Put out nest boxes when it's nesting season, in appropriate and safe places.

- If you find a bird's nest, make sure it is secure, especially if a wind/rainstorm is approaching. If the weather is bad or is going to be bad, it might be a good idea to take the nest down carefully and put in a small box and place it back securely in the same spot it was made. In rough weather, birds' nests can easily fall; if this does happen, it will often kill all the babies.

3. If you find birds (especially baby birds) out of the nest, it can be helpful to know what to do. This will depend on the bird's age and health:

- If you find a baby bird, put it back in the nest if your children removed it.

- If the baby bird has feathers all over its body, except under its wing, put it near some bushes or other covered area, close to where you found it. Be careful not to put it close to a red ant hill or your neighbor's cat.

- If the bird is has few or no feathers, try to find the nest to put it back.

- If you cannot find a nest, call your local wildlife rescue. Many birds are protected species and you require a license to care for them. For example, all but three species in Texas are protected. They may instruct you to feed it wet dog food for a day or two until they can pick it up. Beyond that, pet food stores have formulas for baby birds.

- Many birds put food in the infant's mouth; pigeons are an exception, in that the infants take food out of the parent's mouth. If a baby pigeon is being difficult to feed, find a syringe large enough for the baby to put its beak in after you cut off the front of it. Look online for a home made formula for pigeons; their dietary needs are slightly different.

- A bird that falls off its perch may have a condition called rickets, due a lack in dietary needs. The wildlife group, internet or a bird breeder may have suggestions.

4. If you have found a wild bird that is either an injured bird, or a lost young bird, you can help. If the bird appears to be alive, bring the bird to your house, and place the bird in a container (such

as a shoebox, or something similar). Keep the lid off, as you don't want to suffocate the bird. Don't worry about the bird flying away; it is probably in shock and won't move for a while. As a precaution, if the bird does move, close the windows and doors in the room that the bird is in. Call the local animal shelter or humane society, as they probably know how to take care of birds. If you can, take the bird to the shelter/humane society, and they will deal with the rest. If they cannot take care of the bird, keep it around for a few hours and see if it starts responding to you and flying around. If that happens, it has probably recovered and you should let it out into the wild again. The following articles may be of some assistance:

- Make baby bird rescue food

- Care for an injured wild bird that cannot fly

- Care for a baby bird fallen out of a nest

- Care for a bird that has hit a window

- Rescue a songbird, hawk or owl.

    If the bird dies in the hours that you keep it, tough luck; you can't really do much. Take the dead bird outside and leave it somewhere secluded. Don't bury it unless you are sure that it is legal to do so where you live.

Grooming Pets

Pets require cleaning and grooming. Keeping the surroundings clean where the pet primarily stays is also important. Hygiene is also important for keeping diseases as well as parasites at bay. The aspects elucidated in this chapter are of vital importance, and provide a better understanding of pet grooming.

Dog Grooming

Dog grooming shop in Mons (Belgium).

Dog grooming refers to both the hygienic care and cleaning of a dog, as well as a process by which a dog's physical appearance is enhanced for showing or other types of competition. A dog groomer (or simply "groomer") is a person who earns their living grooming dogs.

Reasons for Grooming

Grooming is a vital part in the well-being and healthiness of a dog which can improve their lifespan. All Breeds require daily grooming, how much depends on the breed, age, or health of the pet. Regular grooming helps to ensure the dog is healthy and comfortable. It is important to note that while many dogs *shed*, others (such as the Poodle), do not shed (see Moult) as profusely, and require grooming by a professional every 6–8 weeks maximum.

The main reasons for daily grooming include:

- decreased chance of various health problems, such as thrush, scratches, and other skin problems

and make the dog look pretty

- general cleanliness of the dog

- monitoring of the dog's health by checking for cuts, heat, swelling, lameness, or changes in temperament, all of which could be indicative of illness

- forging of a closer bond between dog and owner

- reducing infestation load of external parasites on skin.

Grooming a dog using a shedding blade.

Tools and Supplies

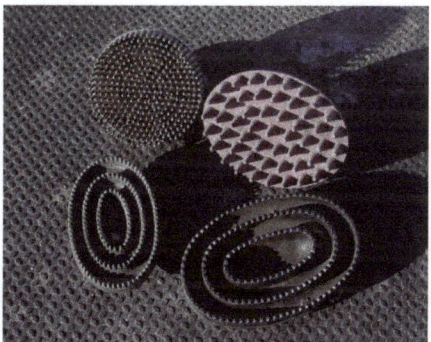
Various types of currycombs

Curry or Curry Brush: A tool made of rubber or plastic with short "teeth." The tool is rubbed (or "curried") over the dog's coat to loosen dirt, hair, and other detritus, and stimulate the skin into producing natural oils. They are more commonly used for dogs that have large amounts of hair that has shed such as for the German Shepherds. They are also used for untangling knots in certain parts of the dog's body such as ears, paws or tail. Using a currycomb must be done carefully as the action of this type of tool can harm the skin of the dog, if pulled too hard.

A shedding blade

Shedding blade: A metal shedding blade with short, dull teeth is used to remove dead hair from certain types of harsh coats. The shedding blade is not used to cut the hair.

Scissors and clippers: Cutting tools used to remove/shorten hair on certain types of coats or in sensitive areas. Not all types of coat are suitable for clipping, i.e. double coats on breeds such as Border Collies keep the dog cool in summer and warm in winter, and should not be clipped unless the dog is matted. The typical pair of scissors for dog grooming is between 6.5 and 9 inches long, longer than typical hair dressing scissors. Some are designed with a blunt tip to prevent any injuries due to the dog moving around.

Stripping Combs/Knives: Tools used to help grab the longer hairs on a harsh coat and pull them out by the root. Helps maintain a proper coat in many terriers and schnauzers. Most often used on show dogs.

Grooming a dog before it is bathed is important as it frees up and removes dead undercoat and matting, and allows proper penetration of water and shampoo to the skin. This can be done by using a slicker brush all over its body, especially on its legs, and the places where knotting occurs frequently. Groomers sometimes use a metal comb when combing for the second time, paying more attention to the toes and between the toes. Metal combs can be helpful in the areas of the dog's body that are common spots for knots. Brushing and combing the tail is also important as it is a commonly missed area.

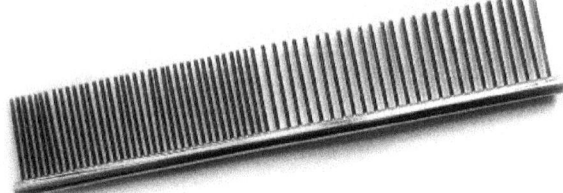

A stainless steel comb to groom dogs with a coarse or fine coat

Dog brushes come in various sizes and shapes can be made from metal, plastic and wood. Although there are many types of dog brushes, they are not very popular amongst the professional dog groomers as most of them prefer using teasels. Dog brushes are perfect for breeds that have long and fragile hair, especially if the coat is getting properly taken care of. Common dog brushes are the bristle brush, wire pin brush, and the slicker brush.

The bristle brush is one of the most widely used types of brushes mainly because it can be used for any type of coat. As a general rule, longer and widely spaced bristles are suitable for dogs with longer coats and shorter and tightly-packed ones are better to use on dogs with short hair. Typically, the bristle brush is used on dogs with long coats to finish the coat and to bring out the natural lustre and shine of the coat. It is commonly used in daily grooming as it removes surface dust and dirt.

Dogs with medium to long hair are often brushed with a wire pin brush. The wire pin brush is also great for dogs with curly coats. They usually have an oval shape and have metal bristles set in a flexible rubber base. This type of brushes is great for dogs with long, wiry, wavy and curly coats as they are useful in separating and untangle the coat. Pin brushes are of better quality if they have polished pins or coated pins which prevent from scratching and harming the dog's skin. Because the coating or polish may go away over time, the pins of such a brush should be replaced once in a while. Pin brushes come in a variety of sizes, textures and fullness, depending on the type of coat that they are needed for.

Slicker brushes are typically used after primarily brushing with a bristle or a wire pin brush. They are used to smooth the coat and to take out mats and tangles. They are provided with fine wire pins that are secured to a flat base. The pins are bent at an angle approximately halfway down the pin. The slicker brush is typically used on dogs with long coats and those with curly coats. For heavier and thicker coats, one is recommended to use a brush with stiffer pins. This type of brush comes in a wide range of sizes and degrees of pin stiffness.

There are also brushes that combine the pin and bristle styles. This type of dog brushes are maybe the most convenient as they have the advantage of having two brushes in one. The combination pin/bristle brush has two different sides, one with bristles which can be successfully used for grooming the short hair areas of the coat, and another side, with pins that can be used for long-coated and double-coated dogs.

Matt combs These are special combs that help to 'cut' matted hair from the dog's coat without leaving a bald spot.

Rakes are important grooming tools especially for double-coated dogs such as the Newfoundlands or Siberian Huskies. They are good in removing dead hair from the undercoat. The undercoat rake's teeth are especially designed to penetrate through the overcoat down into the thick undercoat to remove loose hair faster and easier than a standard comb. Rakes can also be used for untangling and dematting.

The Coat King is a particular type of stripping knives, useful in hand stripping for the removal of dead undercoat prior to clipping. These tools are suitable for many dog breeds and coats and they have become more and more popular among dog owners and groomers. They are a good tool for removing loose hair, and thick undercoats. Also, they can be used for dematting and detangling. Although they are quite a new grooming instrument, they are now widely used and recommended for dog owners.

Stand dryers are also available for a quick drying of the dog's coat. Commonly, when a dog is brought to a groomer this implies a thorough cleaning of the coat as well. And because the dog cannot leave the shop while wet, special driers have been manufactured. These can be stand driers, cage driers or hand driers and are more common in professional grooming places than in the owner's house. Drying a dog with a dryer designed for humans is not recommended as it could cause scalp irritation, dry skin or skin sores.

Shampoos and conditioners are common grooming supplies used by every dog owner. Owners are recommended to use only shampoos, conditioners and rinses that are especially designed for dogs.

Bath tubs are supplies more commonly found in professional grooming shops. They are made of a variety of materials, including galvanized steel. Also, these shops may have bathing systems and sprayers available for a better grooming as well as for the comfort of the pet.

Dog owners who want to groom their pets at home will need ear and eye supplies. Also a variety of combs and brushes for their specific breed of dog. Cleaning the ears and the eyes of the dogs is also part of a complete grooming. Different ear and eyes kits are available on the market and they are especially designed for this matter. They are however meant to be carefully handled and one should not use other products in cleaning the dog's eyes and ears than those that are intended for it.

Dental care may be most important while grooming, just like humans a clean mouth can impact the pets health greatly as it ages. This is however quite a difficult mission, given that dogs hardly allow their teeth to be brushed. The dental kits available on the market include everything from special tooth paste to toothbrushes. Many models of toothbrushes include a three flexible head design which maintains the proper pressure on all surfaces of the tooth with every stroke. These brushes have side bristles set the 45-degree angles to reduce the arm twisting and soft outer bristles for massaging the gums. Toothpaste designed to be used on dogs is usually natural sugar free toothpaste with different flavoring. Foaming or rinsing is not necessary.

Finishing touches can be added with finishing supplies, including perfumed sprays, ribbons and many other accessories.

Flea control products are also part of grooming supplies. There is a wide variety of flea and tick control products that are applied to dogs while grooming. If ticks or fleas are found on the pet, they must be quickly removed and grooming is the perfect time to do it. The specially designed such products must be used for few months in order to ensure that the pet is parasite free.

Grooming tables make the entire activity more comfortable and safer, but they are normally used by professional groomers and owners who have dogs that enter competitive shows. These tables do provide a secure and productive environment for grooming, but many single dog owners can avoid this expense by simply using what is available in the home.

Bathing

Dogs can be bathed by being sprayed with a hand-held shower head, or doused with water from a bucket. Often, one bath will not make a dog truly clean. A second bath is excellent to ensure the entire body has been cleaned. Dogs should be bathed with warm, not hot water, in order to make it a more enjoyable experience. Dogs with a heavy or matted coat should never be bathed without first being completely brushed out or clipped of any mats.

Many types of shampoos and conditioners formulated for dogs are available; however, using a shampoo without mixing it with water may be a bit strong for a dog that's just getting a touch-up bath. If the dog needs a bath, shampoo should be mixed with cold or hand-warm water in the manufacturers recommended ratio to make it easier on the dog and to make sure it rinses entirely. If any shampoo remains on the dog after the bath, it may become irritating to the skin. Most dogs do not require frequent bathing; shampooing a coat too often can strip the coat of its natural oils, causing it to dry out.

Hair Removal

Slicker brush used for removal of loose hair and knots

The coats of many breeds require trimming, cutting, or other attention. Styles vary by breed and discipline. While some hair removal has its origins in practical purposes, much is based on the taste of the owner, whether or not the dog will be shown, and what work the dog does.

A six-month-old Lhasa Apso before and after a visit to a professional groomer.

The rubber grooming gloves and dog brushes are intended to drag loose hair from the short-coated dogs and are some of the most popular grooming tools amongst pet owners. They are easy to use, as using them basically means massaging the coat in firm strokes and have the advantage of being suitable for both wet and dry coats.

Some breeds of dog, such as the Lhasa Apso, do not shed fur but have hair that grows constantly. As such, the fur around the legs and belly can get very long and become matted and the hair around the eyes can impair the dog's vision. In such circumstances, hair trimming can be performed to keep the eyes clear of fur and keep the main body free of knots. However, some owners prefer breeds, such as the Lhasa, to have long, flowing coats that reach down to the floor and will undertake a greater brushing regime than is required for a dog that has its fur kept shorter.

Stripping

The coats of Border Terriers must be stripped. Here an unstripped adult Border Terrier (left) is shown with a puppy.

Stripping or hand-stripping is the process of pulling the dead hair out of the coat of a non-shedding dog, either by using a stripping knife or the fingers. A hard, wiry coat has a cycle where it starts growing and then sheds as it reaches maximum length. Hand-stripping coordinates the shedding and makes room for a new coat to grow. Stripping is the proper grooming method for most terriers, spaniels, and many other breeds. The hair is removed with either a stripping knife or stripping stone, with the top coat removed to reveal the dense, soft undercoat. If done correctly, the procedure is painless. Many dogs are reported to enjoy having their hair stripped, especially when they are introduced to it as puppies.

The body of this adult Border Terrier has been stripped.

Nail Trimming

Nail trimming is essential for maintaining good health. If a dog's nails are allowed to grow, they will curl over into a spiral shape; walking will become increasingly painful to the dog as they grow, putting pressure on the dogs toes (a bit like walking in shoes that are too small). Uncut nails may curl so far that they pierce the paw pad, leading to infection and debilitating pain. If one does not trim a dog's nails on a monthly basis the quick will grow along with the nail, making it nearly impossible to cut properly. Owners may choose to trim nails themselves or may opt to take their pet to a groomer or veterinarian.

Nail trimming is done with a nail clipper. There are three main types of nail clippers, the guillotine clipper,standard scissors nail clipper and the file trimmer.

Creative Grooming

Additional options that some groomers provide include services such as colouring dogs' fur and painting dogs' nails.

While traditional grooming achieves to conform with breed standards set by the official breed associations, creative grooming heads to the opposite direction, creating a unique, sometimes exquisite look.

The lighter version of creative grooming is known as pet tuning and is more owner-oriented, adjusting the pets' visual appearance to their owners' amusement or life style, while the creative grooming is more of an art form, therefore more artist (groomer) oriented.

Other Services

Groomers may also sell products for dogs' fur and other products such as dog clothing.

How to Groom a Dog

Regular grooming keeps your dog clean, healthy, and comfortable. Many people prefer professional groomers; they can make dogs look great while using their professional expertise to keep them safe. However, if you don't have one available in your area or just want to save some money, you can give your dog a basic grooming at home.

Part 1

Grooming your Dog Before the Bath

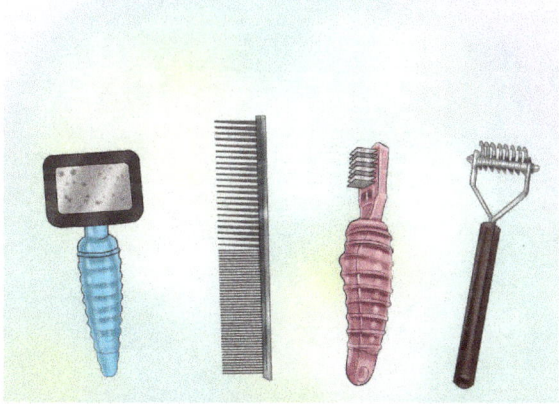

1. Gather your grooming materials. You don't want to be looking for your tools once you begin grooming your dog. Make sure to have everything you need in one place before you begin the task at hand. Consult the "Things You'll Need" section below to find out what you'll need to groom your dog.

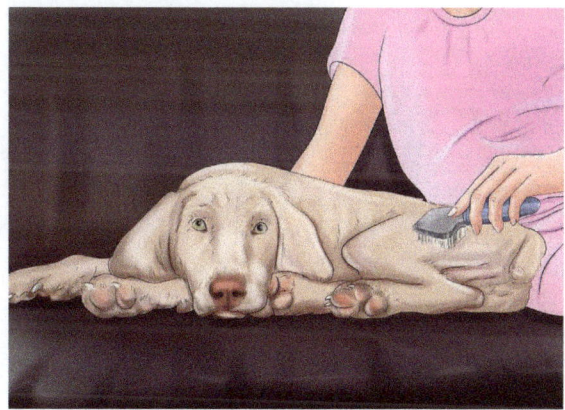

2. Comb out your dog first. Combing your dog's coat daily or every other day will keep most mats at bay. Simply brushing, as most literature instructs, is not enough for dogs that can mat up: the brush will easily pass over at angles that a comb will get stuck on. A thorough combing should always be the first step of the grooming process because any mats will become tighter and less manageable once they dry. Begin on the head and move down the body. Be careful under the belly, as it is a sensitive area, and don't forget to comb the tail.

- While you are combing, if you find a tangle, use a brush and try to work out the tangle. Be mindful not to brush burn your dog from brushing for too long in the same spot. You can check by looking under the fur to see if the skin becomes red with irritation.

- You can brush short-haired dogs with simple tools like curry brushes or gloves.

- Comb and brush medium- to long-coated dogs with more specialized tools like a steel comb, slicker, a pin brush, or an undercoat rake.

- Whatever you use, it must remove loose hair and distribute oils from the skin throughout the coat.

3. Praise your dog as you're brushing. Reward calm, quiet behavior to encourage more of it. You may want to include a treat to reward the dog for good behavior.

4. Give the dog breaks as needed. You don't want the dog to get overwhelmed; any negative associations can make grooming harder in the future. Make the experience fun by giving your pet breaks from time to time, giving praise, treats, pets, and even a little bit of play. This will also keep your dog distracted.

- This is especially important with a puppy, which can be trained from a young age to tolerate this much handling well.

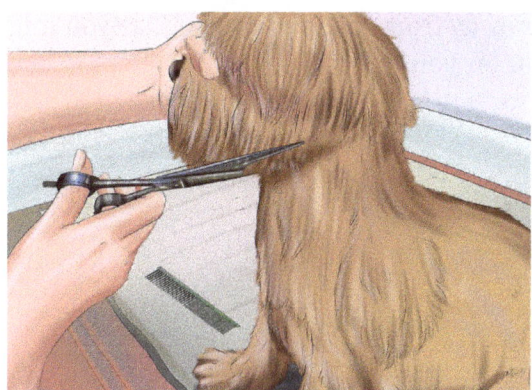

5. Cut out mats that can't be brushed out. Severe matting can pull the skin every time the dog moves, making daily life painful for your pet. If you can't brush a mat out, you need to either cut or shave it off, depending on how close it is to the skin. Be extremely careful if you use scissors to avoid injuring yourself or your pet. Try to cut parallel to the growth of the hair to avoid a choppy look.

- If you don't think you can safely remove the mat without hurting your dog, take him to a professional groomer.

- On occasion, mats can get so tight and close to the skin that bacterial infections occur underneath the mat. If you suspect an infection, take your dog to the veterinarian as soon as possible.

- The visual symptoms of bacterial infection are redness and moisture, with pus secretion in advanced cases. You dog might chew or scratch at the area because it itches.

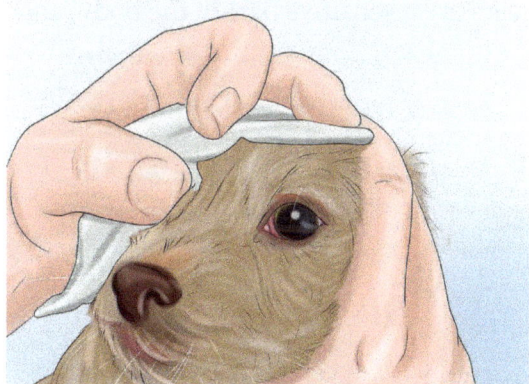

6. Clear the dog's eyes. White-haired breeds or those with large eyes that water a lot (Pekingese, Pugs, Pomeranians, etc.) may need more maintenance in this area than others. Depending on your particular dog, this step may be a simple matter of wiping or pulling eye debris away from the corners of the eyes. Long-haired or white-haired dogs may need special attention to make sure that all gunk is out of the coat, as they may get tear stains. You can buy products made for removing "tear stains" from a white coat at a pet supply store.

- A healthy eye should be clear and should not show any signs of irritation or unusual discharge.

- Don't try to trim hair away from the eyes yourself, as you might injure your pet. Ask your vet or groomer to do it for you.

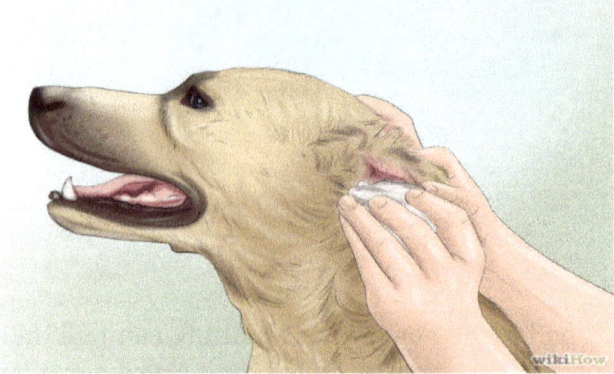

7. Clean your dog's ears. It's normal for a clean ear to have some wax in it, but there shouldn't be any particular smell to it. To clean your dog's ears, apply some ear cleaning solution (bought at a pet supply store) to a cotton round. Not too much or it will drip into the ear while wiping. Wipe dirt and wax away from the inner ear, but don't rub vigorously, as this might cause sores. Don't push too far into the ear, either. If your dog has drop ears like a bassett hound, wipe the inside of the ear flag as dirt collects there as well. The groomers rule of thumb is to clean only what you can see.

- Bring ear cleaning solution up to body temperature before putting it in the dog's ears. Place it in a body-temperature water bath, just as you would with a baby bottle.

- When you're done wiping out the ear with a damp cotton ball or cloth, gently dry it out with a dry one.

- Praise your dog! The ears are a sensitive part of the body, and he may need some comfort.

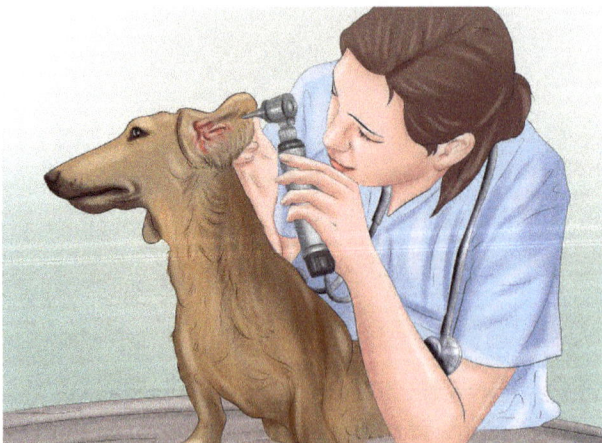

8. Contact the vet for ear problems. Your dog needs medical attention if his ears look swollen, red, irritated, dark or blackened. Any discharge or sores, or a bad or yeast like smell should also prompt a call to the vet.

- Excessive discharge, inflammation, one ear is much dirtier than the other, and odor are signs of an ear infection that need medication.

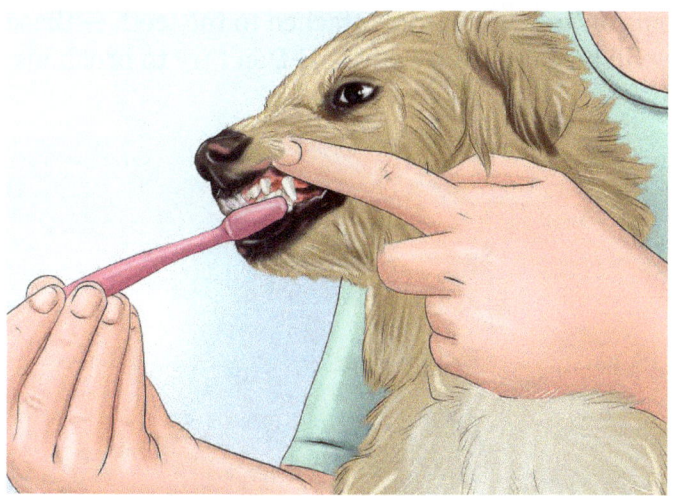

9. Brush the dog's teeth. Ideally, brushing your dog's teeth every day with dog toothpaste is the route to healthy teeth and gums. Use dog toothpaste instead of human products, so you don't poison your dog with fluoride. If there is any chance that you may get bitten by your dog, do NOT attempt to brush your pet's teeth. At any point, if the dog gets overwhelmed, give him a break to calm down.

- Start by placing a small amount of dog toothpaste on your finger and spreading it across the teeth for a few seconds. Reward the dog for cooperating.

- Once the dog lets you work your finger in his mouth for 20-30 seconds, you can graduate to gauze or finger toothbrushes from the pet store. Work your way up to a dog toothbrush.

- No matter what, ease your dog into the process so that it can be a pleasant experience rather than a stressful one.

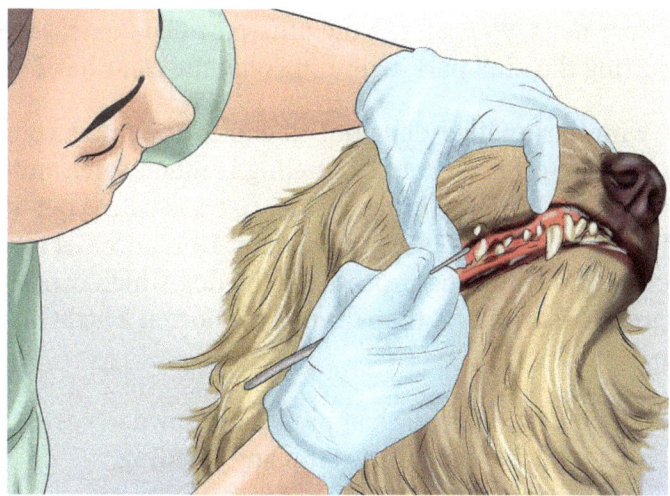

10. Get a veterinary cleaning if necessary. If your dog already has a considerable buildup of tartar and plaque, a simple tooth-brushing won't be enough. Just like a human would, your dog needs a professional cleaning at the veterinarians. Another option is anesthesia-free teeth cleaning, which is available but typically not offered by veterinarians.

- Look for red gums or brown material attached to the teeth — these are signs that a home tooth-brushing will be painful for your dog. Don't try to brush his teeth until he's seen a vet.

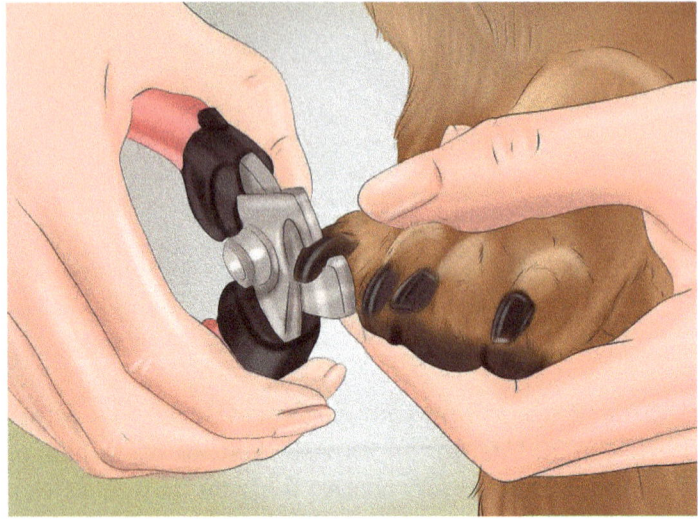

11. Clip the dog's nails. If left untrimmed, a dog's nails can curl under into the paw pads or twist toes in a way that causes joint damage. To keep your dog's nails short, clip them regularly, depending on how fast his nails grow. If you can hear his nails on the ground when he walks, that means his nails are touching the ground, and are too long.

- Trim a very small amount of nail (1/16 inch) away with a pair of dog nail clippers. Human clippers are okay for a very young puppy or small dog. Guillotine style clippers are less effective than the scissor type. Also, use the appropriate size clippers for your dog.

- If your dog has clear nails, you can see the pink part (The quick) where the blood vessel's located. Avoid cutting the pink part, trimming only the clear hard nail.

- Take extra care with dark-nailed dogs not to clip to the quick (blood vessel). Go slowly, and only take a little bit off at a time. Dremeling is much safer and easier to avoid hitting the quick, as it shaves only a little bit at a time. Use a cordless pet-safe Dremel tool, as the corded ones will not stop turning if they catch hair. Don't dremel for too long as it will burn the nail and prolong the trimming process for the dog which causes more stress. The best recommended process is trim first then dremel to shorten a little bit and round out the nail do it's not sharp.

- If you cut too far and hit a blood vessel, apply styptic powder, cornstarch, or flour with a bit of pressure and hold for a few seconds to stop any bleeding.

- For most dogs, this is the worst part for them. Some people do this step last to avoid the dog immediately becoming too stressed to do much grooming afterward. If trimming nails last and quick the nail, you can wash just the paw with a little water or wipe it off with hydrogen peroxide to get the blood off after applying blood clotting substances.

Part 2

Bathing your Dog

1. Gather your supplies. You don't want to be running around looking for cleaning products with a wet dog in the tub, so have everything in one place before you start. You should also make sure that you're properly dressed in clothes you don't mind getting messy because you *will* get wet. At the very least, you will need:

- Dog shampoo

- Treats

- Several towels

- Place one towel on the edge of the tub to keep water from splashing over the tub. The rest are for drying.

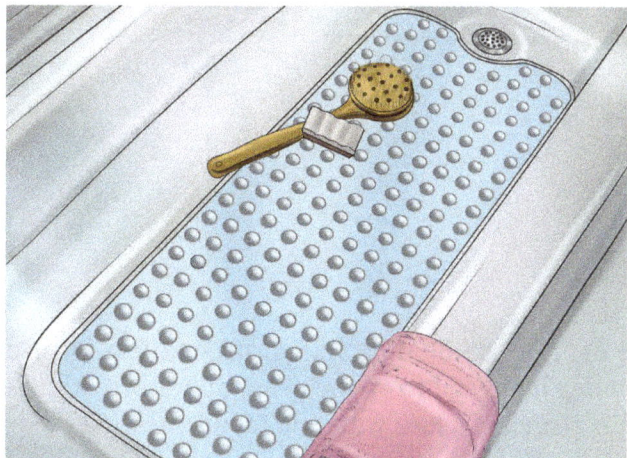

2. Place a non-slip surface on the bottom of the tub. You know from experience that the tub can get slippery once it gets soapy. To prevent your dog from slipping, place a towel or non-slip bath mat in the tub.

3. Run shower with lukewarm water. Hot water can harm your dog's skin, especially if your dog is short haired. Avoid running water right away on the dog, as it may cause unnecessary stress and burns if starts out hot without checking first. You may have to spend some time desensitizing your dog to the sound of running water with the help of his favourite treats. Always go slowly to avoid overwhelming your pet and making things worse for both of you. If you only have a tub and no shower, use a hose outside as filling a tub with water or only have a cup to run over the dog with water will not penetrate the fur or completely rinse off shampoo properly which causes infection as well as dry skin if completely soaked in water. This is true for even short hair dogs like pit bulls, you don't need the high power setting of any hose only enough to not hurt or stress the dog but still gets the job done.

- Read your shampoo directions carefully as some have specific dilution instructions. If you can't find any such directions, then use as is for diluting too much may affect how clean the dog will be. Some shampoos are for treatment of fleas and ticks ONLY, they're not for prevention so it's advised to not use them for a normal bath.

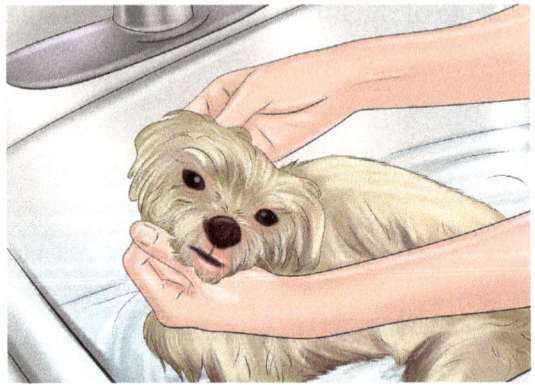

4. Secure the dog in the bathtub. Some dogs like to make a run for it during bath-time. If this describes your dog, buy a dog bath lead from the pet supply store. It's a leash that attaches to the shower's wall with a suction cup and keeps your dog in place during the bath.

- Replace the dog's regular collar with one that will not stain the coat or suffer water damage. A slip lead that adjusts to a struggling dog is best but the dog may choke itself no matter the restraint so monitor his breathing carefully and adjust or simply push them back when necessary.

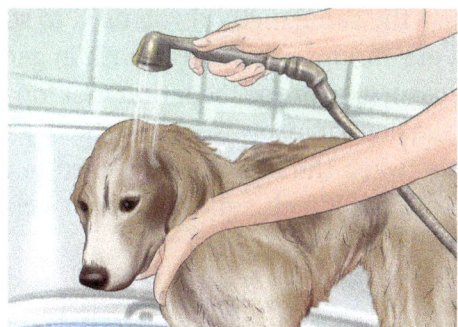

5. Soak your dog thoroughly. Make sure your dog's coat is completely wet before you start applying shampoo to it. If your dog isn't afraid, you can buy and use a hose and water pressurizer attachment for the faucet. This is especially helpful if you have a large dog or one with a double-coat. AVOID getting water in your dog's ears. Water in the ears can cause an infection. Please be sure to only spray water/rinse water up to the dog's neck. The head can be cleaned separately (see below for instructions).

6. Shampoo the dog. Begin at the neck and move downward toward the rear and legs, using your fingers to spread the shampoo and work it in down to the skin. Save the head for last, and don't use soap around the ears and eyes(unless you have tearless shampoo meant for dogs). Instead, use a wet towel or washcloth to clean the head.

- Once the shampoo is applied, running a rake or rubber curry brush through a double-coated dog's coat will help to loosen it and better distribute the shampoo - just be careful not to rake one spot for too long.

- Shampoos may be easier to apply and rinse off if diluted properly.

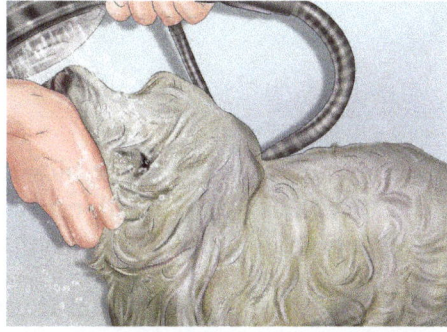

7. Rinse your dog thoroughly. As long as you see dirt or soap bubbles in the water coming off of

an area, keep rinsing. You can use the same method you used to soak the dog's coat before shampooing. If your dog is too afraid of running water or the bath in general and can't be done on your own, there are veterinarians who can give proper sedation, not too much, to allow you to groom in a couple of hours or can groom the dog themselves. Touch the dog all over to feel for any shampoo especially the chest area and inbetween the legs they are hard to get. To test you the rub the fur inbetween you fingers and pull softly, if it feels squeaky then it's clean.

8. Dry your dog. Use a squeegee or use your hand as a squeegee to force water off of the coat and body. Towel dry him as best as you can while he's still in the tub, so you don't make a mess. Place the towel over your dog's back, or hold it next to him and give permission to shake the water off their body. Many dogs will learn the "bath rules" and wait to shake until you have placed the towel over them to contain the water droplets. Another type of towel to use is a chamois, which is a thin fleece like towel that is designed to be wrung out when wet. It lessens the amount of towels needed and does the bulk of the work. Using a chamois, then a towel makes drying less of a hassle.

- If you have a double coated or long-haired dog, you may need to blow the coat dry.

9. Blow dry the dog if necessary. If towel drying won't cut it, blow-drying can dry the coat without overheating or over-drying your dog. If you have a dog with especially long hair, you may need to dry the coat while brushing it. Towel drying along with blow drying is the fastest method.

- Make sure that the blow dryer is on the cool setting! It may take longer than usual, but it's worth the time because there will be less of a chance your dog's hair and skin will dry out.

- If your dog is afraid of the sound or sensation of the blow dryer, don't push him. Towel-dry him as best as possible and let him air dry somewhere he can't make a mess, like a laundry room. Don't allow the dog out completely wet as the water will cause irritation and dryness if not at least towel dried first.

Part 3

Clipping your Dog's Fur

1. Decide if you need to clip your dog's coat. Many breeds have short hair and don't require regular clipping. However, if you have a shaggier breed of dog, he may require regular clipping as part of his health routine. Breeds that need regular coat trims include cocker spaniel, sheepdog, poodle, collie, Shih Tzu, Pekingese, and chow chow, among others.

2. Clip the dog's fur after it's completely dried. If you plan to clip your dog's hair, make sure to read the directions that came with the clippers. Get an information book or video, or consult with a groomer about the proper use of your clippers. Make sure that the clipper blades are sharp and the clippers well lubricated. If the blades are not sharp, they can pull on the hair.

- Before clipping your dog, you should have an idea of the look you are trying to create. Read, ask questions and watch videos to get an idea of how to achieve the desired result.Then you may start.

3. Restrain the dog gently. You don't want him moving around, so tie him up with a leash. During the clipping process, you can place your free hand under the dog's belly to encourage him to stay in place instead of fidgeting. If the dog is nervous, keep praising him in a calm voice or sing. Healthy treats are also good to have.

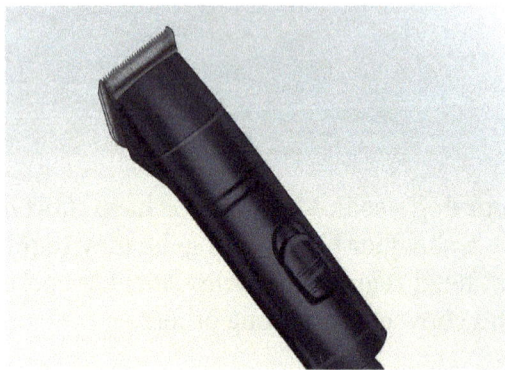

4. Use dog grooming clippers. It's worth it to spend a little bit of extra money on a good pair of dog grooming clippers. A small investment up front will save you money down the road, since you won't have to pay professionals to groom your pet.

- Make sure to use dog grooming blades that will give you the coat length you desire.

- Scissors will likely not give you a nice, even coat, and you may hurt the dog with them if he moves suddenly. Grooming clippers are recommended over scissors.

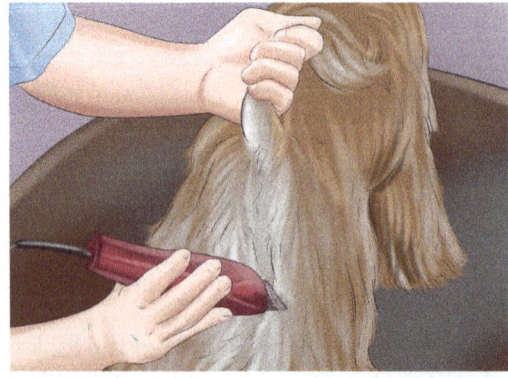

5. Clip the dog's hair methodically. You can place the blade against the body safely, so long as you

don't press the blade strongly into the skin. Brush against the direction of hair growth(back-brush) before running the clippers the other direction; with the direction or hair growth. Using the clippers against the growth of hair will have the same effect as back-brushing, but will leave a shorter length than the clipper blade that you are using. If you want to shave against the growth of hair, a blade size gets two blade sizes smaller when cutting against the grain. For example, when cutting with 4# against the grain check how long a 7# leaves behind when cutting with the grain. Move the clippers surely, but slowly across the dog's body to remove the hair — moving too fast might leave uneven lines. Always move the blade with the direction of the hairs' growth unless you want a shorter length than your blade claims to leave. Begin at the neck, then move down to the shoulders, under the ears, and toward the chin, throat, and chest areas. DO NOT use a size seven or any skip blades around the throat area or any flaps on the body that can fit between the teeth, such as the Achilles' tendons, arm pits, genital area, tip of tail, or anus. Then, clip the dog's back and sides. Finally, clip the hair on the dog's legs. Be careful when cutting the neck with any blade as it's the most dangerous to cut. Never cut straight down, do so at angles to avoid flaps you can't see in the neck getting cut.

6. Be careful when removing hair around the anus. The anus can pop out, like a button, unexpectedly and be accidentally cut as a result- anticipate this action. Don't run the clippers over the anus, only outward from around the anus and under the base of the tail. Treat your clippers like a pencil.

- Be careful when clipping around the legs, tail and face. These areas can be sensitive. The dog will also dodge around and may end up cutting themselves by jerking so fast.

- Check the clippers frequently to make sure they don't get hot enough to hurt your dog's skin. If the clipper blades do get hot, stop and use a product like "Clipper Lube" spray on them.

7. Reward your dog. Standing still can be hard work! If he seems like he's getting overwhelmed by

all this handling, give your dog a break every few minutes. Praise him throughout the process, and give treats during the break. Do not play with the dog where there is a chance for him to get dirty or too excited to stand still during the process again.

8. Be patient. You may have to go over your dog's coat a few times before you have a smooth, even cut. Don't rush it! Give your dog as many breaks as necessary, and make sure to move your clippers slowly. Brushing up against the coat then going the spot with clippers again help to get a smooth cut. Do will have to be done many times before you are done.

How to Groom a Cat

Cats are generally very clean pets and groom themselves. But some cats may not be able to adequately groom themselves, such as when they have fleas or very long fur. But by maintaining your cat's coat and caring for her other hygiene needs such as clipping her claws, you can keep your cat groomed.

Part 1

Maintaining your Cat's Coat

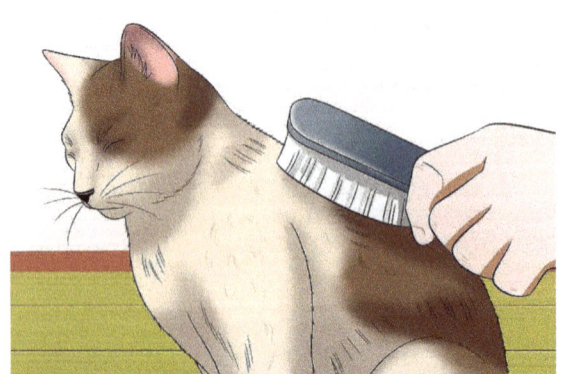

1. Brush your cat's fur. Cats have either short or long hair. Even though a cat will groom her own

fur, brushing it keeps her coat especially lush by removing dirt, grease, and dead hair. In addition, brushing your cat can be a wonderful bonding experience for the two of you.

- Use a cat-specific metal comb or rubber brush to brush your cat. Brush your kitty once or twice a week, or more often if she is a longhair type, or if she is shedding a lot, to keep her coat glowing.

- Keep in mind that cats generally don't like to be restrained. Approach her slowly and hold her gently while you brush your cat. You can also brush her when she is sleeping or sitting in your lap but be careful not to wake her up, brush her gently but not too gently.. just normal!.

- Brush slowly so you don't startle your cat. Give her praise or treats as you continue brushing her.

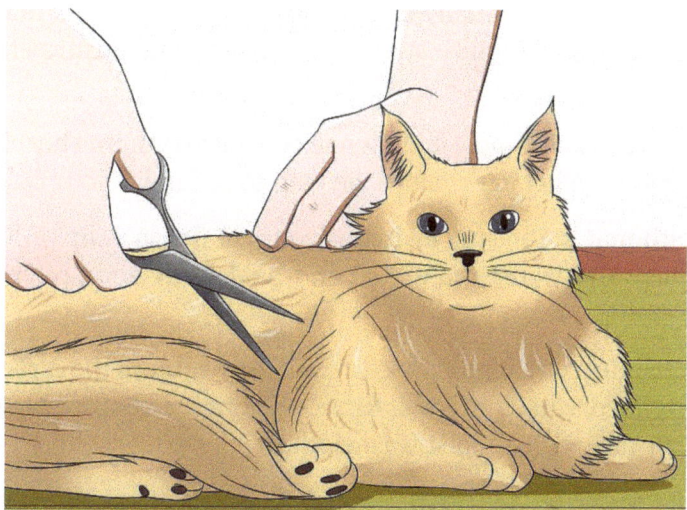

2. Clip your kitty's fur. Most cat's will never need their fur clipped or trimmed. However, your kitty may need clipping or trimming in some cases, such as she has long fur that is matting, which can cause health problems. Trim or clip your kitty's fur only if it is absolutely necessary or consider allowing a professional groomer to clip her fur.

- Use only clippers for animals and take frequent breaks so you don't burn your kitty's skin.

- Use gentle pressure when clipping your cat. Lightly guide the clippers along your cat's body. Leave at least an inch of hair, which can prevent hair growth problems and skin issues.

- Be very careful around the cat's ears, anus, genitals, underbelly and legs so that you don't hurt your cat.

- Touch up with or use scissors if you prefer.

- Consider hiring a professional cat groomer to trim your pet's fur. Remember that cat's don't enjoy being restrained, which may lead to injuries if you decide to clip her. Ask your vet if she offers these services or can recommend a professional cat groomer.

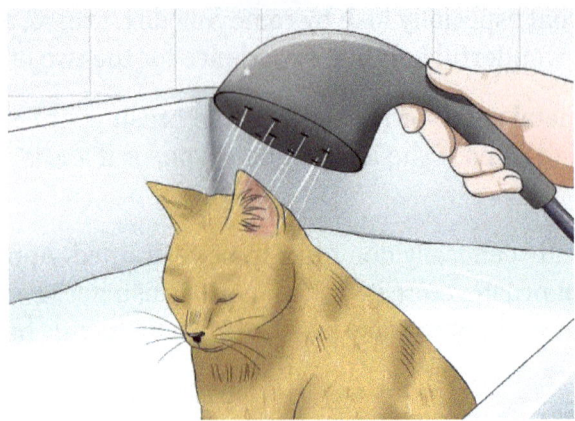

3. Bathe your cat. Although you cat's tongue and teeth are built-in grooming tools that can tackle her fur care needs, you might occasionally need to bathe her if she gets into something sticky or stinky. Following these tips can minimize stress to your kitty and ensure efficiency in getting out the offensive matter in her fur:

- Give her the bath when she is most mellow and consider trimming her claws, brushing her and placing a bit of cotton in her ears before the bath to minimize your risk of getting scratched.

- Put a rubber bath mat in the sink or tub so your cat doesn't slip. Fill the sink or bath with 3-4 inches of lukewarm water and use a hand-held spray hose, pitcher, or cup to wet your kitty.

- Massage her with one part cat shampoo to five parts water in the direction of her fur growth and avoiding her face, ears, and eyes. Rinse off your cat thoroughly with lukewarm water before wiping her face with a moist washcloth.

- Wrap her in a large and let her dry in a warm place. You can use a hair dryer on the lowest setting if your cat doesn't mind.

- Make sure to offer her lots of praise and treats for a successful bathing session.

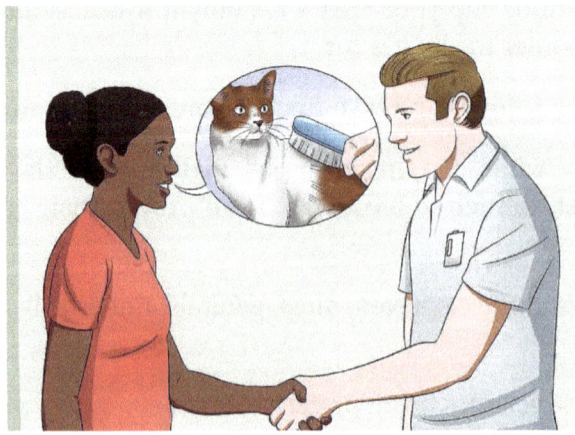

4. Visit a professional cat groomer. If you don't have the time or patience to care for your cat's fur or hygiene, consider hiring a professional groomer. Be aware that this can be expensive, but can save you time and be less traumatic for your cat.

- Your local vet, humane society, or the American Society for the Prevention of Cruelty to animals can suggest local groomers for your cat. You can also ask friends and family members for recommendations.

- Consider visiting groomers' businesses before you send your cat. This will let you get a sense of the facility and see if the groomer is kind to your cat.

Part 2

Addressing Problems while Grooming

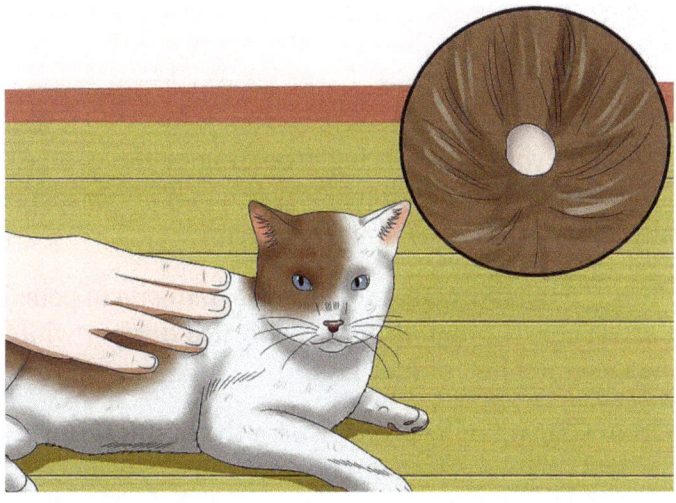

1. Check for skin problems. Whenever you brush, clip, or bathe your cat, check her skin for bumps, bald spots, or cuts. This can indicate health problems such as allergies or stress. See your vet if you find any strange or unexplained anomalies on your cat's skin or fur. Some skin problems your cat may have are:

- Parasitic infections from fleas, ear mites, or harvest mites

- Fungal infections such as ringworm or yeast infections

- Infections from excess bacteria on the skin

- Viral infections such as feline cowpox

- Feline acne or seborrhea

- Immune disorders such as allergies and feline eosinophilic granuloma complex

- Sun damage like skin cancer

- Contact dermatitis

- Drug reactions

- Fur loss due to stress

- Trauma from accidents or collars.

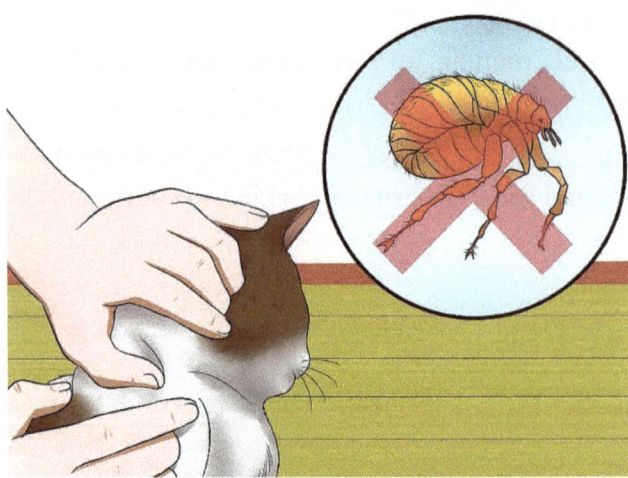

2. Kill fleas. If you find fleas on your kitty during grooming or the course of caring for her daily, you'll need to get rid of them as soon as possible. Fleas can make your kitty itch, lead to skin problems, or even other health issues such as having tapeworms.

- Recognize that fleas are the most common external parasite in pets. They feed on the blood of your cat and are visible through droppings of "flea dirt" or white flea eggs on your cat, persistent itching or scratching, or hair loss.

- Get a diagnosis from your vet of fleas and ask for the best treatment of them. Your vet may suggest topical or oral treatments, shampoos, sprays, or powders.

- Follow the packaging instructions and make sure to not use medication on your cat or any other pets unless it is designated for that specific animal. Be aware that you'll need to treat other animals in your home and thoroughly clean your house to help get rid of fleas and their eggs.

- Consider treating your lawn if your cat goes outside.

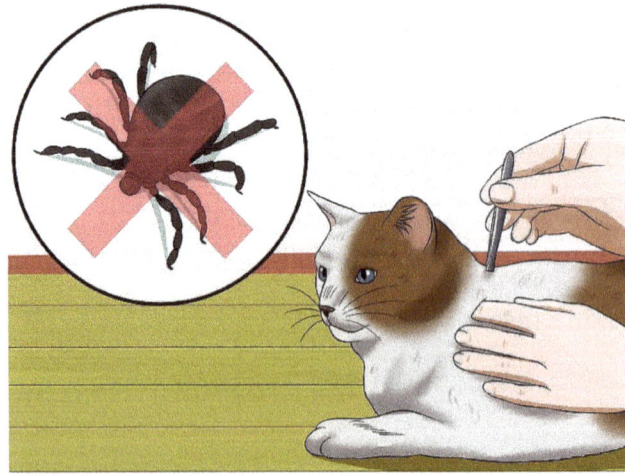

3. Remove visible ticks. Another common parasite that cats who go outside can get are ticks. These arachnids can spread serious diseases to your cat, so check her whenever your groom her or she

comes indoors. Remove the tick and take your cat to the vet to ensure that she doesn't have any further ticks or tick-related conditions.

- Be aware that most ticks are visible to the naked eye. They are about the size of a pinhead but swell as they feed on your cat's blood.

- Put on a pair of rubber or latex gloves and grasp the tick with a pair of tweezers. Pull straight upwards in a steady motion and place the tick in a jar of rubbing alcohol for veterinary testing.

- Disinfect the area of your cat's fur with soap and water, wash your hands and tweezers, too.

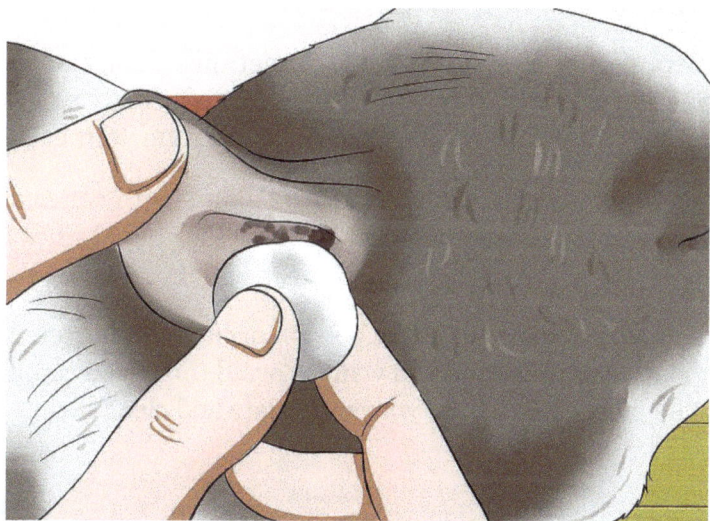

4. Get rid of ear mites. Tiny parasites called ear mites are also common in cats, though mostly in kittens and younger cats. They are highly contagious and can lead to skin and hearing problems.

- Recognize ear mites by a black, coffee ground-like discharge in your cats ears.

- Take your cat to the vet to confirm a diagnosis of ear mites. The vet will give you treatment to get rid of the mites and soothe your cat's itchy ears. She may also suggest ways to clean your cat's ears if you suspect mites in the future. Follow any instructions the vet gives you for medication.

- Be aware that ear mites are highly contagious and other animals in your home will also require treatment.

- Clean mites from your kitty's ears by wrapping her in a towel when she is calm and holding her earflap out with one hand. Use your other hand to squeeze out a cotton ball drenched in ear cleaner at the opening of her ear canal. Use ear cleaner specially-formulated for cats that you can buy either at a pet store or get from your vet.

- Release your cat, which may result in some shaking and dislodging of debris. After a few minutes reassure your cat and wipe any debris from her ears with a dry cotton ball. Repeat the process in the other ear.

5. Take care of problem scents and substances. Sometimes your cat might get herself into something, such as paint or a skunk, that leaves her especially dirty or in need of a bath. Taking care of these problems as soon as possible can help maintain your cat's health and hygiene.

- Flush the eyes and mouth of a cat sprayed by a skunk with water and give her a bath if necessary. If the spray was heavy, take her to her vet for blood work to ensure she doesn't develop anemia.

- Bathe your cat as soon as possible if she gets oil or paint on herself. Cats are naturally inclined to lick themselves clean and you want to avoid this if you can. If your cat has a lot of oil on her fur, you may want to have your vet sedate and clean her.

Part 3

Caring for your Cat's Hygiene

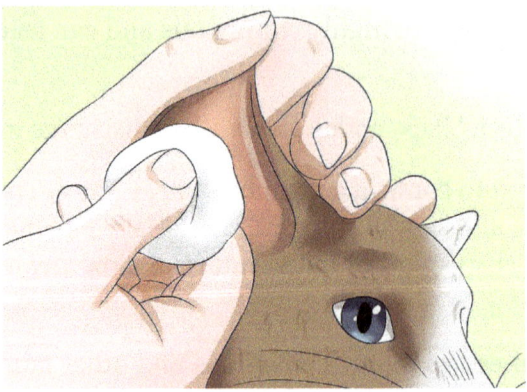

1. Monitor your cat's ears. Your kitty should get routine checkups at a vet, which includes checking on the health of her ears. But in between vet visits, it's important to check your kitty's ears once a week for wax, debris, or infection.

- Check her outer ear flap, or pinna, to make sure it has no bald spots and that its inner surface is clean and light pink.

- Examine her inner ear by folding back each ear and looking down into the canal. Make sure there is no debris, odor, and minimal ear wax. The color should be light pink.

- Use a cotton ball dampened in liquid cat ear cleansing solution. Fold back your cat's ear and gently wipe away any debris. Avoid probing or poking anything into the ear canal, which can cause trauma or infection.

- Take your cat to the vet if you notice any discharge, caked wax, redness, swelling, bleeding, or unpleasant odor.

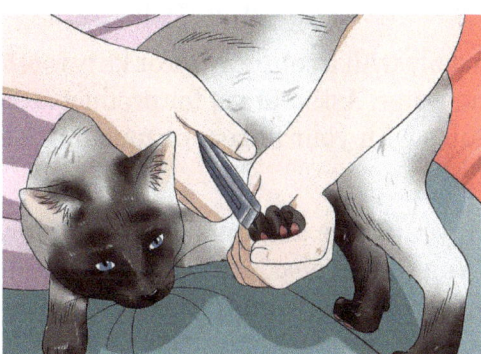

2. Trim your cat's nails. Every few weeks, your cat may need her nails trimmed. This helps prevent breaking, infection, and an irregular gait because her nails are too long.

- Use only a nail clipper designed for cats. Purchase this item a pet store or your vet's office.

- Wrap your kitty in a towel to prevent her from scratching and/ or ask a friend to hold your cat while you clip her nails.

- Trim your cat's nails slowly and methodically so you minimize the risk of hurting her. Avoid clipping too close to the quick, which is the blood vessel inside of the nail. Clip above this area and hold your cat's paw firmly and cut the nail in a single stroke.

- Use a clotting agent if you accidentally cut the quick.

- Give kitty a treat for a successful nail clipping session.

- Avoid forcing your cat to endure trimming. Ask a vet or groomer to clip the nails to prevent injury to your cat—or you.

- Remember that your cat needs to scratch to maintain the health of her paws. Offer her a scratching post and check her paws for wounds.

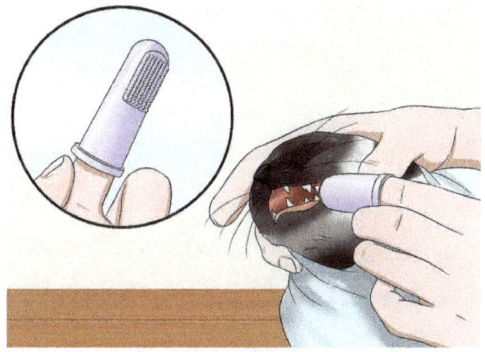

3. Maintain kitty's oral health. Every cat needs clean, sharp teeth and healthy gums. Dental

disease is a common problem seen by veterinarians. Checking your kitty's mouth and keeping it clean with brushing and regular vet visits can help keep disease at bay and your cat's breath fresh.

- Push back your kitty's gums gently when she is facing you during daily oral care. Make sure her gums are firm and pink and not swollen. Her teeth should be clean and free of brownish tartar and show no signs of being loose or broken.

- Brush your kitty's teeth daily with a cotton swab or kitty toothbrush and a feline toothpaste. You can also use salt and water. Ask your vet for product recommendations. Start by gently massaging your cat's gums with your fingers or touching a cotton swab to them and then proceed to the cleaning.

- Take your cat to a vet if you notice abnormally strong odor, which can indicate digestive problems or gingivitis. You should also look out for dark red lines along the gums, red and swollen gums, mouth ulcers, loose teeth, difficulty chewing food, excessive drooling, or pawing at her mouth.

- Remember to praise and soothe your kitty for good behavior while brushing.

How to Groom a Rabbit

Rabbits require regular grooming. You will need to brush your rabbit every few days to remove loose fur and prevent hairballs Long hair breeds require more grooming than shorthair breeds in order to keep their fur clean, glossy, and free of matts.. Regular cleaning and even bathing is necessary in domestic rabbit ownership. Rabbits naturally clean themselves like cats, but they may not be able to do the job if they are overweight or otherwise impaired.

Method 1

Brushing a Rabbit

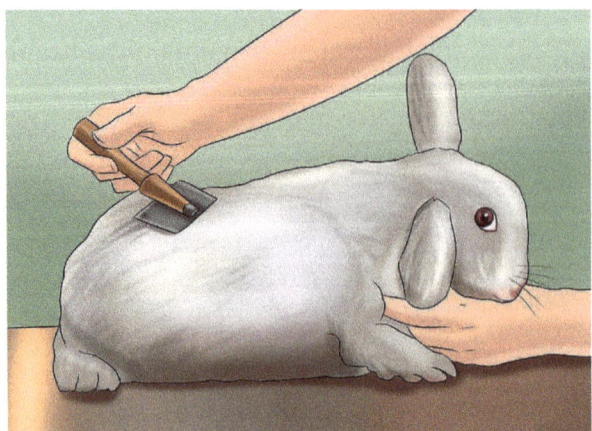

1. Brush your rabbit at least once a week. The first function of this is removing loose fur. Long-haired varieties like the Angora need to be brushed every day or two. You only need to brush short-

haired breeds like the Netherland Dwarf once a week. Gently and thoroughly brush the rabbit's back with a soft-bristle brush. This will bring loose hair to the top of the coat.

- Always brush in the direction of the fur, and do not brush too hard. Be careful not to hurt the rabbit!

- Use a pin brush for basic brushing, and a wide-toothed comb for rabbits with long fur. A bristle brush makes a good once over to smooth the fur and get any extra shed hair. A mat rake will help remove tangles that are too big for the other brushes.

- Brush using a pin brush or wide toothed brush, depending on your rabbit's fur. When the brush stops picking up shed hairs, use the bristle brush to collect the rest.

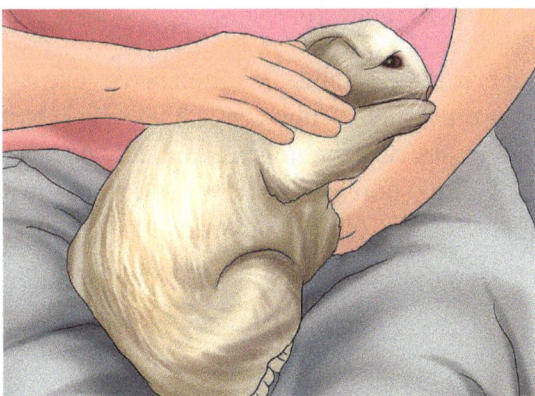

2. Make your rabbit comfortable. Brushing is the first step to making it feel at ease, but there are additional techniques. Lay a towel over your lap and gently support it along the length of your thighs. Rabbits love to lay on their backs while you slowly brush their tummies and underarms. This can send rabbits into a relaxed, sleep-like state. It might even make little noises of satisfaction.

3. Adjust your brushing regimen for the time of year. Brush your rabbit more often when it's shedding. Rabbits shed about every three months. They tend to shed most heavily in the fall and spring, and comparatively lightly during the summer and winter. Rabbits shed a few different ways.

- Some rabbits take a few weeks to lose their old coat of fur. You may need to brush your rabbit every few days or multiple times each day depending on its coat length and how quickly it sheds.

- Other rabbits shed their entire old coats within a day. It is especially important that you do not neglect these rabbits once they start shedding.

4. Understand the important of brushing. Rabbits lick themselves like cats to keep clean, and they can get hairballs if they consume too much hair. Unlike cats, however, rabbits are physically incapable of vomiting. Hairballs can cause stomach obstructions and quickly become life threatening by blocking the stomach exit. Remove loose hair as soon as possible or your rabbit will do it during grooming.

5. Remove more fur with water. Wet your hands with the spritzer bottle and gently stroke your rabbit from behind the ears all the way back to the tail. Make sure to do this several times, stroking the sides and belly of the rabbit as well. Your wet hands will help remove the excess fur that your brush brings to the top of the coat. You can often remove a very large percentage of the loose hair by just pulling it out with your hand.

6. Remove the last bit of excess fur. A wire-slicker brush is the best way to get the last bit out. This is especially important during shedding season, when the rabbit is both losing and producing more

fur. Use your wire brush to remove mats and tangles, then use a softer brush to stroke along the grain of the fur. Never brush the fur against the grain, or the wire brush will severely damage your rabbit's fur.

Method 2

Cleaning a Rabbit

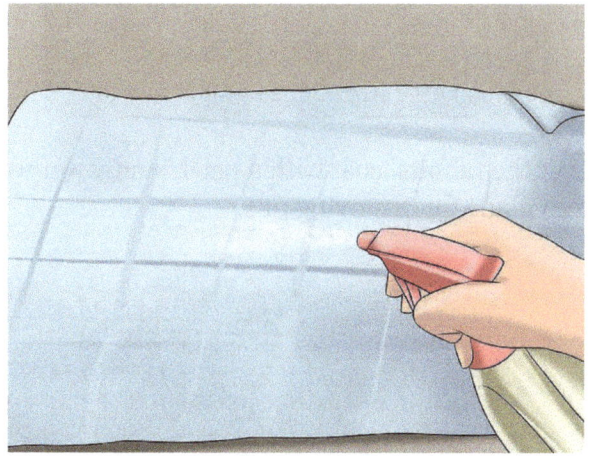

1. Prepare your rabbit for the bath. Moisten a clean towel with a grooming spray. Use the towel to wipe dirty spots on the rabbit. Do not use soap on your rabbit, unless the product is specifically made for rabbits.

2. Clean the rabbit's rear end. Use a clean towel or wet-wipe to wipe off any crusted feces or debris. This will help prevent any illnesses that might result from unsanitary conditions. If there are feces stuck to your rabbit's fur, it is usually because your rabbit is overweight and unable to clean itself. Take your rabbit to a vet and ask about weight-loss options.

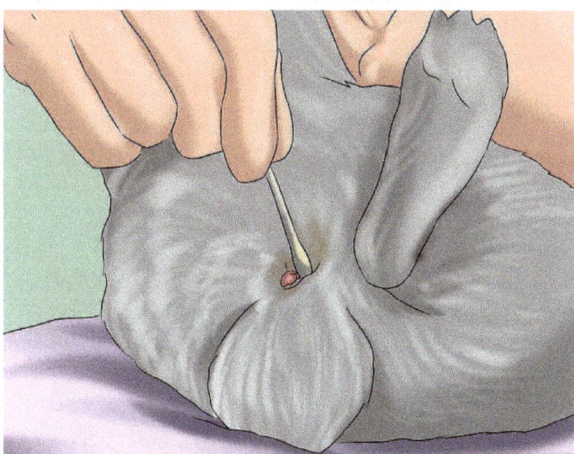

3. Clean your rabbit's scent glands. Find these just above their bottom when you are holding them upright. To clean the scent glands out, get a cotton bud and wet it with warm water. You may need someone to help you hold the rabbit securely upside down. Gently swab the scent glands until any discharge comes off. If you have any trouble doing this, ask your vet to do it for you.

4. Wipe the fur clean. Go over the rabbits' coat with a pet-friendly wet wipe. If your rabbit tends to be oily, try pet-friendly wipes made for removing oils.

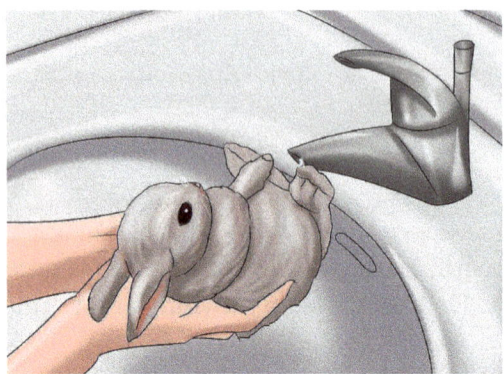

5. Bathe in moderation. Only bathe your rabbit if it is extremely dirty or has soiled itself. Fill your sink or a small tub with clean, warm water, and slowly wash your rabbit without dunking it completely. Wash everything except for the face and the ears. Then, soap up your rabbit with the rabbit shampoo. Make sure to scrub the legs and bottom to remove all the feces. Then, drain your sink, and rinse your rabbit off.

Method 3

General Grooming and Handling Tips

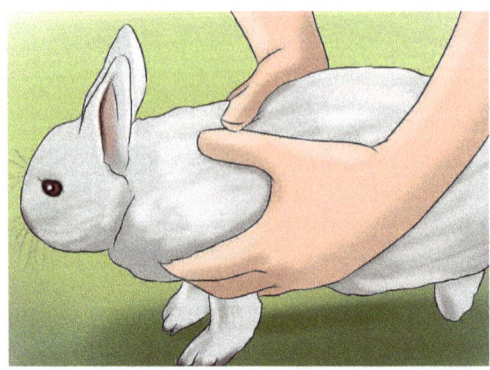

1. Be gentle with your rabbit. Pick your rabbit up carefully, and hold it tightly so that it cannot

thrash around. Restrain the rabbit by wrapping it snugly in a towel, like a burrito. Leave only the head exposed. A struggling rabbit is difficult to handle, it could even break its back. Rabbits are very social creatures. You should have few issues with handling your bunny as long as you spend quality time bonding with it.

2. Keep the rabbit's eyes free of fur and hay. This will help prevent the irritation and potential infection of your rabbit's eyes. Use moist cotton balls to gently clean the area around the eye. If your rabbit has a heavy amount of fur around its eyes, try using a mascara brush or a small flea comb to comb back the fur from the eye.

- Never directly touch the rabbit's eye. This can cause more harm than good.

- If there is something in the rabbit's eye, take it to a veterinarian or look for a rabbit-approved eye wash solution. You may be able to wash the surface of the eye with focused water drops from an eye-dropper.

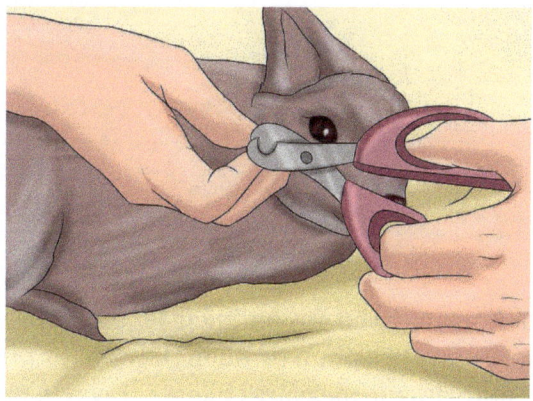

3. Clip your rabbit's nails. Rabbits need their claws trimmed every 4-6 weeks. The claws are like fingernails, and never stop growing. Most indoor rabbits won't wear their claws down enough, so they need to be clipped before they grow out of hand. Hold your bunny on its back like you would cradle a baby, then gently clip its nails. Be cautious not to cut too far, as this will cause immense pain and bleeding in the rabbit. You can buy a special rabbit nail clipper to make this process easier, or you can (very carefully) wield a standard human nail clipper.

- Try to make it a good experience with treats so your rabbit will be more comfortable with you handling its feet.

- Make sure to only trim the white part of the nails. Leave the pink roots (the blood vessels) alone! It helps to shine a light from underneath the claw so you can ensure that you don't clip the blood vessel. If you clip the blood vessel apply styptic powder or flour to help clot the bleeding. Apply pressure for about a minute.

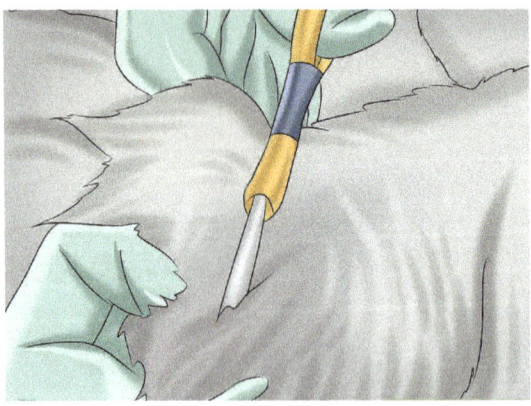

4. Trim your rabbit's fur. If your long-haired rabbit that keeps developing hairballs and matted fur, try cutting the fur down to an inch or so. You can use scissors or a pair of standard trimming shears. This way, the rabbit won't get cold, but it will be much less likely to develop loose hair.

- Do not trim the fur all the way to the skin. Fur offers natural protection against heat, cold, and anything that may injure the rabbit.

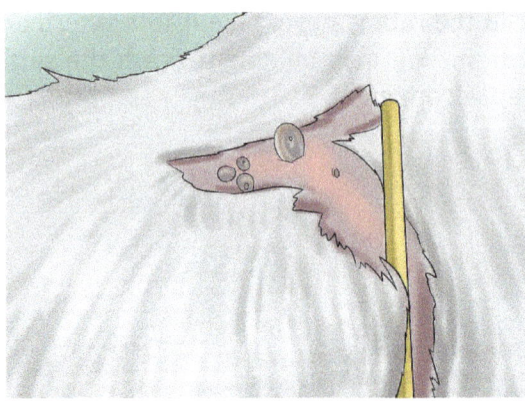

5. Check for fleas. If your rabbit seems to be scratching itself more than normal, try splaying its fur to check for fleas. If you do notice any fleas, run through the rabbit's fur with a flea comb to remove them. You may need to take more drastic measures like a spray or a flea collar.

How to Clean a Fish Tank

Keep your fish happy and healthy by cleaning their tank and adding fresh water once a week. Cleaning an aquarium isn't difficult, especially if you make sure to do it on a schedule so algae and other residue doesn't have time to build up. This article explains how to clean a freshwater or saltwater aquarium.

Method 1

Freshwater Aquariums

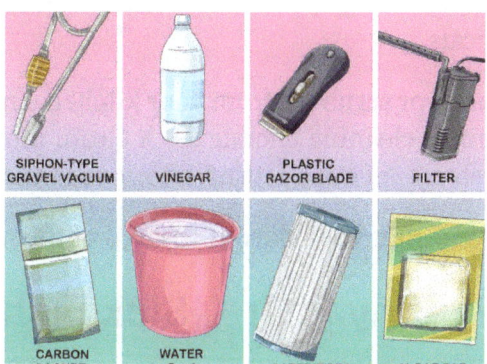

1. Get your cleaning supplies ready. Run through your checklist and ensure that you've prepped your tools and your workspace.

- Properly prepared water in the quantity you'll need to replace.

- An algae pad for cleaning the glass inside the tank.

- A large bucket (5 gallons or 10 litres, and bigger) dedicated for this purpose.

- A simple siphon-type gravel vacuum (NOT a battery-operated gadget).

- Filter media (cartridges, sponges, carbon packets, and so on) if you're changing the filter this time.

- Aquarium-safe glass cleaner or a vinegar-based solution.

- 10% bleach solution in a separate container (optional)

- Metal or plastic razor blade (optional, be careful with acrylic tanks, as these scratch easier)

- Also, Make sure that if your fish are pretty picky eaters, you put some water cleaner in with siphoning the water. Siphon half the tank one week, then do the other tank 2-3 weeks later. This will help your fish adjust to a cleaner climate.

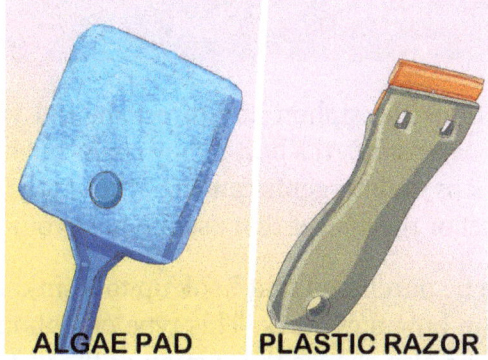

ALGAE PAD   PLASTIC RAZOR

2. Clean the sides of the aquarium with the algae pad. Run it along the glass, scrubbing a little as

necessary, to remove algae that is sticking to the aquarium. If you come across a particularly difficult patch of residue, use a razor blade or plastic blade to scrape it off the glass.

- You might want to wear rubber gloves to complete this job. Make sure they haven't been treated with any chemicals.

- Do not just use the sponge or scrubber from your kitchen sink or anything that could have the residue of detergent or cleaning chemicals. A clean, tank-only algae pad will prevent harsh chemicals and detergents from getting into your tank.

- This step can also be done after you take out 10-20% of the water.

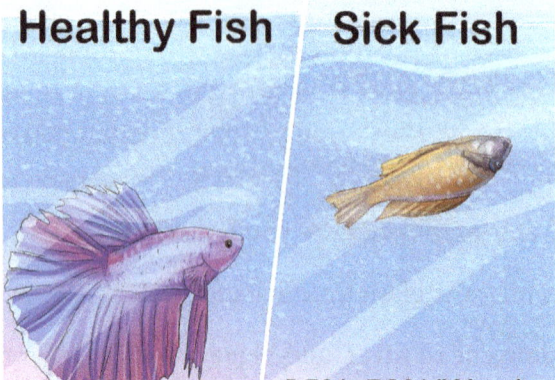

3. Decide how much water you are going to change. If you clean your tank on a regular schedule and if your fish are healthy, changing 10-20% of the water once a week should be plenty. If you have a sick fish, you'll want to change more of the water - at least 25% to 50%.

4. Siphon out the old water. Start the siphon and direct the old water into a pail, preferably a five-gallon bucket (or larger if necessary). It's best to buy a new bucket and use it only for cleaning your fish tank; residue from soaps or detergents can be harmful to your fish. This means no repurposing the laundry room bucket or the bucket that used to hold your dishwashing cleaning agents.

- Aquarium siphons can be purchased that hook up to a sink. If you have one of these, read over the instructions on how they work. This type of siphon also prevents water spilling from the bucket. You can also choose the suction of the water and the temperature when filling the tank using the taps.

5. Clean the gravel. Push the gravel vacuum through the gravel. Fish waste, excess food, and other debris will be sucked into the the vacuum. If you have very small, weak, or delicate fish, you can put a never-worn stocking over the end of the syphon (but be sure the mesh is large enough to get the debris).

- If you have sand substrate, do not use the vacuum like a shovel. Use just the hose part of the siphon, not the plastic tube, holding it under an inch from the surface to suck up waste without disturbing your sand. You can use your fingers to run through the sand (provided there are no buried animals to disturb)to help gunk float up that might have gotten trapped under shifting sand.

6. Clean the decorations. Tank decorations need cleaning, too! Excess algae is caused by excess nutrients in the water. You can wipe the decorations off with an algae pad or a never-used soft-bristled toothbrush in the tank water you siphoned out. Avoid the use of soap; it could harm your fishy friend!

- If you're having difficulty cleaning the decorations, remove them from the tank and soak the items in a 10% bleach solution for 15 minutes. Then pour boiling water over them and let them air dry before replacing them in the tank. Be very careful to remove all bleach, as to not kill your fish.

- If your decorations are covered in algae, you may want to feed your fish less or change the water more frequently.

- Having a pleco in larger tanks can prevent algae from growing excessively.

7. Add fresh water. Replace the water you took out with fresh, treated water at the temperature of the aquarium. A thermometer is the way to verify the temperature. Staying inside the dictated temperature parameters is crucial for the health of your fish. Remember, lukewarm is too hot for most fish.

- If you use tap or faucet water, conditioning the water to remove heavy metals and other toxins that your fish can't process is a must. The easiest thing to do is plan ahead; an old milk container works great. Fill it up the day before and leave it uncovered; one day will allow the chlorine to evaporate and the water to become room temperature, the same as your tank. If you are impulsive, a drop of Decleor will do the trick. Just make sure the temperature is the same. A significant change in temperature will kill your fish.

- If the nitrates are astronomically high, you can do a special water change of 50% to 75% with distilled water (not normally recommended because the water is so purified, there are no trace nutritional elements for the fish to soak up). You can also use bottled spring water for water changes (with no conditioner) because this water has none of the bad and all of the good elements.

8. Consider adding aquarium salt for fresh water. Many fish (including Mollies, guppies and platies) live longer and healthier lives. Fresh water aquarium salt also helps to prevent diseases such as ich (Ichthyophthirius multifiliis).

9. Watch the water. Wait a few hours for any cloudiness that remains to dissipate, leaving the water sparkling clear. Although there are water clearing agents on the market, try not to use them. If the water remains cloudy, it's because of an underlying problem and the agent will only mask (not solve) the issue. Don't forget that your fish need some space between the water and the top of the tank, so that they have enough oxygen-carbon dioxide exchange to breathe and so that they can extend their top fin comfortably.

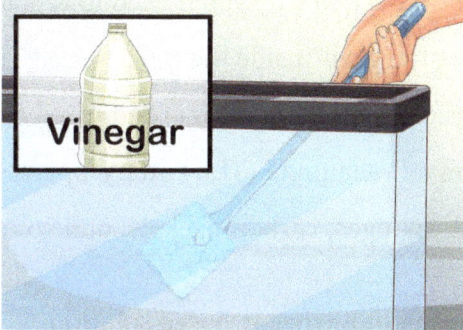

10. Clean the exterior. Wipe down the outside, including glass, hood, light and tank top. The ammonia fumes from standard cleaners can hurt your fish, so only use solutions that are designated as aquarium-safe. If you'd prefer to make your own cleaner, you can use a vinegar-based solution.

11. Change the filter cartridge about once a month. The carbon inside of the filter cartridge can become detrimental to your fishes' health if left unchanged. Not much beneficial bacteria lives inside the filter, most is in the gravel, so changing it will not affect the biological filtration in any way. The cartridge can be rinsed off weekly when water changes are performed if it appears to be excessively dirty, but you don't want to lose whatever bacteria does happen to set in in the filter. Rinsing the filter cartridge does not substitute changing it, so it still has to be changed monthly.

Method 2

Saltwater Aquariums

1. Get your cleaning supplies ready. Saltwater aquariums have special needs in addition to the basic supplies you'd use for a freshwater aquarium. Gather the following supplies:

- Properly prepared water in the quantity you'll need to replace.

- An algae pad for cleaning the glass inside the tank.

- A large bucket (5 gallons or 10 litres, or bigger) dedicated for this purpose.

- A simple siphon-type gravel vacuum (NOT a battery-operated gadget).

- Filter media (cartridges, sponges, carbon packets, and so on) if you're changing the filter this time.

- Aquarium-safe glass cleaner or a vinegar-based solution.

- Salt mix.

- pH strips.

- A refractometer, hygrometer, or salinity probe.

- A thermometer.

- 10% bleach solution in a separate container (optional)

2. Clean off the algae. Use the algae pad to remove algae residue from the inside of the tank. Use a razor blade or plastic blade to scrape off built-up residue that's difficult to remove.

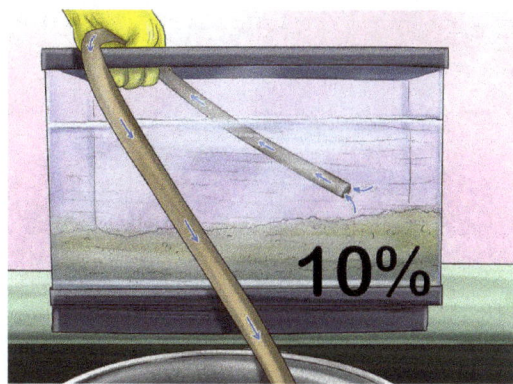

3. Siphon out the water. For a saltwater aquarium, change 10% of the water every 2 weeks. This should be sufficient to eliminate nitrates from the water. Turn on the siphon and let the water run into a large bucket.

4. Clean the gravel. Push the gravel vacuum through the gravel. Fish waste, excess food, and other debris will be sucked into the the vacuum. If you have very small, weak, or delicate fish, you can put a never-worn stocking over the end of the siphon (but be sure the mesh is large enough to get the debris). For sand substrate, use just the hose part of the siphon, not the plastic tube, holding it under an inch from the surface to suck up waste without disturbing your sand.

5. Clean the decorations. Wipe the decorations off with an algae pad or a never-used soft-bristled toothbrush in the tank water you siphoned out. You can also remove the decorations from the tank and soak the items in a 10% bleach solution for 15 minutes. Then pour boiling water over them and let them air dry before replacing them in the tank.

6. Check for salt creep. When the salt water evaporates at the top of the aquarium, it will leave behind a crusty residue known as salt creep. Clean it off with an algae sponge and add back the lost water.

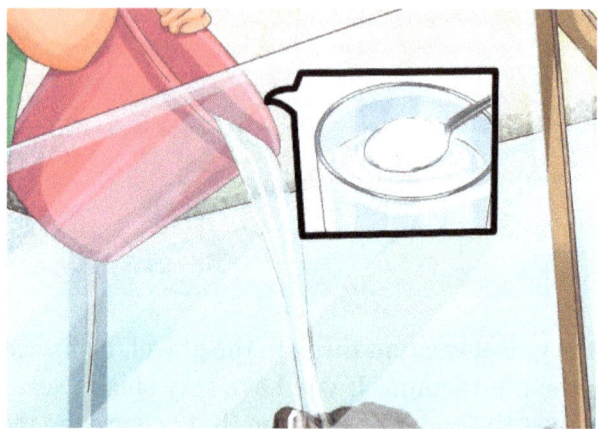

7. Mix a saltwater solution and add it to the tank. Adding water to a saltwater aquarium is a little more involved than the process for a freshwater aquarium. You need to ensure that the temperature, salinity and pH of the water are all within an acceptable range for your fish. Start this process the night before you clean your tank.

- Buy distilled or reverse osmosis water. You can purchase these at the grocery store. Place the water in a clean plastic bucket, preferably used only for this purpose.

- Heat the water with a specialized heater, purchased at a pet store.

- Add the salt mix. One-step salt mixes are available at pet stores. Follow the instructions on how much to add based on how much water you are using. The rule of thumb is 1/2 cup of mix for every gallon of water.

- Let the water aerate overnight. In the morning, check the salinity with a refractometer, hygrometer, or salinity probe. The ideal reading is between 1.021 and 1.025. Also, check the temperature with a thermometer. For saltwater fish, it should be between 73 and 82 degrees Fahrenheit (23 and 28 degrees Celsius).

8. Check the temperatures every day. Saltwater fish live in a relatively narrow temperature range. To make sure they're healthy, you'll want to check the temperature of the aquarium on a daily basis.

Permissions

Index